FERGUSON
CAREER BIOGRAPHIES

HILLARY RODHAM
CLINTON
First Lady and Senator

Bernard Ryan, Jr.

Ferguson
An imprint of ☑® Facts On File

Hillary Rodham Clinton: First Lady and Senator

Copyright © 2004 by Facts On File, Inc.

Ferguson
An imprint of Facts On File, Inc.
132 West 31st Street
New York NY 10001

Ryan, Bernard, 1923–
  Hillary Rodham Clinton: first lady and senator/Bernard Ryan, Jr.
    p. cm.
Summary: A biography of the New York senator and wife of the forty-second president of the United States. Includes information on how to become a lawyer, federal or state official.
Includes bibliographical references and index.
  ISBN 0-8160-5544-0 (alk. paper)
  1. Clinton, Hillary Rodham—Juvenile literature. 2. Presidents' spouses—United States—Biography—Juvenile literature. 3. Legislators—United States—Biography—Juvenile literature. 4. United States. Congress. Senate—Biography—Juvenile literature. [1. Clinton, Hillary Rodham. 2. First ladies. 3. Legislators. 4. Women—Biography.] I. Title.
  E887.C55R93 2004
  328.73'092—dc22   2003022888

Text design by David Strelecky

Pages 111–142 adapted from *Ferguson's Encyclopedia of Careers and Vocational Guidance, Twelfth Edition*

Printed in the United States of America

MP FOF 10 9 8 7 6 5 4 3 2 1

This book is printed on acid-free paper.

CONTENTS

1

READY FOR A GREAT ADVENTURE

On November 7, 2000, the voters in the State of New York elected a woman as the new senator to represent them in Washington, D.C., for the next six years. She was not only the first woman ever elected to the Senate from that State, but she had resided in New York for only 10 months before her election. At the time of her election she was also the nation's first lady, the wife of the president of the United States. Her name was Hillary Rodham Clinton.

What made Hillary such a strong political candidate that millions of voters would want to elect her? One of the most likely reasons is that she is a do-gooder. She has wanted to improve all kinds of things and has been pushing for one reform or another ever since her college days. When the end of her time as first lady was near, she might have returned to her profession as a lawyer. She might have appeared on the lecture circuit, where she could have charged extremely high fees for making speeches at conventions and corporate meetings. Or she might have taken an executive job with a powerful and wealthy foundation dedicated to good works. But instead, Hillary Rodham Clinton tackled the tough world of New York State politics. Even though most experts thought she would lose, Hillary believed that as a senator she could do more to make changes

than she could in any other way, and she was determined to win the office.

New York U.S. Senator-elect Hillary Rodham Clinton cele-brates her victory with daughter Chelsea and President Bill Clinton, Nov. 7, 2000. (Associated Press)

Proud and Straitlaced Parents

During the Great Depression of the 1930s, Hillary's father, Hugh Rodham, played football and majored in physical education at Penn State while earning college money by working in a Pennsylvania coal mine. For four years after college, he was a curtain salesman in Chicago. During World War II he served as a Navy chief petty officer teaching physical education. He married Dorothy Howell, a secretary at the curtain company, in 1942. Their first child, Hillary Diane, was born on October 26, 1947.

Soon after the war, Hugh Rodham started his own business in Chicago. He made draperies for hotels and corporate offices, printing and cutting the cloth himself, then sewing and installing it. His wife served as bookkeeper for the business. In 1950, they paid cash for a yellow-brick Georgian house in Park Ridge, a well-to-do suburb northwest of Chicago. Hillary's brother, Hugh Rodham Jr., was born that year, and another brother, Anthony, arrived in 1954.

The Rodhams were proud and straitlaced. Hillary's father drove a Cadillac, chewed tobacco, and expressed strong opinions to anyone ready to argue politics with him. Watching his sons play baseball, he sat in his own folding chair far down left field from the crowd in the grandstand. When Hugh Jr., quarterback of his high school football team, completed 10 out of 11 passes to win the conference championship, his father greeted him with, "I got nothing to say to you, except that you should have completed the other one."

Hillary was nearly four when her family moved to the Park Ridge house. Day after day, she went out to play in the neighborhood, then came home in tears. One girl whom the boys admitted to their gang was beating up on Hillary to keep her from joining the group. Finally, Hillary's mother told her, "There's no room in this house for cowards. The next time she hits you, I want you to hit her back." Soon Hillary reported, "I can play with the boys now."

Hillary's mother had always told her daughter that school was a great adventure in which she would learn great things. By fifth grade at Eugene Field Elementary, Hillary Rodham was such a good student that, the following year, her teacher also moved up to sixth grade so she could teach Hillary for another year. But when Hillary brought home straight-A report cards, her father's only comment was, "You must go to a pretty easy school." Still, he taught her how to read stock tables and how to hit a curveball in school softball games.

While a schoolgirl, Hillary earned many Girl Scout badges and was a competent athlete in tennis, soccer, softball, and table tennis. Entering high school, she was a wading-pool lifeguard with her junior life-saving certificate and was earning spending money as a baby-sitter.

Hillary Rodham (standing) poses with high school classmates in 1964. (Associated Press, Park Ridge HS)

An Active Student

In Park Ridge's Maine East High School, Hillary was a strong competitor in her studies and activities. She worked hard not only to land on the honor roll but to earn places on the prom committee, the "cultural values" committee, and the student council. Her classmates had strong opinions about her. To some, she seemed too serious and distant. Others thought her bossy. But everyone agreed that she was one of the most mature and active members of her class, and she had a reputation for expressing herself well and getting things done.

Park Ridge was a staunchly Republican community. During the presidential campaign in 1964, Hillary headed the membership committee of her high school's Students for Barry Goldwater, who was running against incumbent Democratic President Lyndon B. Johnson. In a debate, she was required to represent Johnson's side. She later recalled that she "had to study all these positions and I had to learn things from a different point of view, not just what my father had said or what my community believed. That opened me up to looking at things from a different point of view."

The "University of Life"

The first strong nonfamily influence in Hillary's life was the Reverend Don Jones. In the summer of 1961, when Hillary was 14, Rev. Jones arrived at First Methodist, the Rodhams'

A busy student takes a break in the sunshine. (Wellesley College Archives)

church, as a new minister just out of seminary. As a young minister, Jones was excited about breathing new life and fresh ideas into this formal community. He took charge of the youth group, renaming it the "University of Life" and introducing the young people to the poetry of T. S. Eliot and e. e. cummings, the music of Bob Dylan, and such films as Francois Truffaut's *The 400 Blows*.

That summer, Hillary got older students from First Methodist's Bible school to baby-sit for the children of migrant workers on the farms beyond the Chicago suburbs. Jones chauffeured Hillary and her friends to the camps in his sporty red convertible, a car with which he enjoyed startling the town.

Jones took the church youth group to Chicago on April 15, 1962, to hear a sermon by the Rev. Martin Luther King Jr. Titling his address "Remaining Awake Through a Revolution," King said many Americans were Rip Van Winkles, sleeping soundly while great social changes occurred. It was just how Hillary had heard Jones describe Park Ridge. Next, Jones took the University of Life to Chicago again to hear a radical organizer named Saul Alinsky, who would soon become one of Hillary's influential mentors in college.

Thus, Don Jones was instrumental in opening Hillary's eyes and mind to the world beyond Park Ridge. She not only heard the messages of Martin Luther King and Saul Alinsky; she acted on them by reaching out to the larger community through charitable works. For example, she took lemonade and cupcakes to minority children whose parents were cultivating and harvesting the fruit and vegetables for Chicago markets. She also tutored these children and sewed their clothes and their dolls' clothes. Through the children, Hillary learned much more about the vastness and diversity of the human race.

2

MAKING CHANGES AT WELLESLEY

Wellesley College was founded near Boston, Massachusetts, 95 years before Hillary Rodham arrived as a freshman in the fall of 1965. Wellesley had long been one of the "Seven Sisters"—the leading U.S. private colleges for women. The college maintained strong traditions: Students were expected to dress in skirts for dinner. A strict curfew kept them indoors at night, except when weekend dates could last as late as midnight. Every student had to sign an honor code—called "the vow"—promising not to disobey regulations set forth in the student handbook. Wellesley tradition and curriculum expected the college's graduates to become well-adjusted housewives before they became anything else.

In the United States in 1965, however, times were changing. Americans were protesting the Vietnam War.

President Lyndon Johnson had started his Great Society plan for domestic reform in education, civil rights, and economics. Long-pent-up hostilities among the races led to the emergence of the civil rights movement. In 1962, Students for a Democratic Society (SDS) had launched the idea of student power, and in 1964 the free speech movement had spread rapidly from the University of California at Berkeley to campuses nationwide. Across America, students were "sitting in"—literally occupying administrative offices and disrupting college functions as they demanded changes in curriculum and campus government.

A Leadership Role in Making Changes

Such was the broad picture in the United States and at college after college when Hillary Rodham entered Wellesley. She lost no time in adopting this spirit of reform and protest. She took a leadership role in a campaign to end the curfews and get rid of the honor system at her school. At her own expense, she had BREAK THE VOW lapel buttons made. She led a fight to reduce the number of required courses and insisted that Wellesley students have the option of seeing their work graded on a pass-fail basis. Finding only six African-Americans among her 400 classmates, she demanded the admission of larger percentages in future classes and challenged the administration to hire minority professors. She even found time

Hillary Rodham in 1965
(Wellesley College Archives)

to work on a committee charged with revising the system that checked out library books.

During freshman year, Hillary was elected president of Wellesley's Young Republican Club. The club consisted of liberal Republicans who supported the campaigns of New York Congressman John Lindsay for mayor of New York in 1965 and African-American Edward Brooke for senator from Massachusetts in 1966. But during her first two years of college, Hillary was changing her mind about the Republican Party. The main influence for this change was the Vietnam War. Hillary had studied closely the history of the Vietnamese and their country's geography and had become strongly opposed to the war. Thus, in her junior year she quit the Young Republicans, organized a student strike protesting the war, and started working to support the antiwar candidate, Eugene McCarthy (who later dropped out of the race), in his bid for the Democratic nomination for president.

On April 4, 1968, Hillary's frustration with the state of the country reached its peak when she heard about the assassination of Martin Luther King Jr. Her roommate saw Hillary rush into their room in tears after receiving the news. Slamming her bookbag against the wall, Hillary shouted, "I can't stand it anymore! I can't take any more!"

In June of 1968, at home in Chicago, Hillary sat in the gallery of the Democratic National Convention and watched in alarm as Chicago police beat up antiwar protesters her age. Then, over the summer, despite her leanings toward the Democratic Party, she kept a commitment she had made to Wellesley's Washington internship program. She served in the House of Representatives' Republican Conference. At the Republican National Convention, she worked with liberals who wanted to nominate New York's antiwar governor, Nelson Rockefeller, rather than Richard Nixon, for president.

Hillary returned to Wellesley for her senior year, where she was elected president of the student government. She was also completing her major in political science—the study of governmental processes and institutions. She decided to write her senior thesis on the Community Action Program (CAP), a major part of President Johnson's Great Society. The CAP provided federal money for states and cities to set up new agencies to help the poor get politically organized. Many of its ideas had first come from the long-time radical thinker Saul Alinsky, whom Don Jones had taken Hillary to see when she was 14.

Alinsky's reputation dated from the 1930s, when he created the Back of the Yards Council, a pressure group that worked to improve conditions in the slum neighborhoods that encircled the Chicago stockyards. Alinsky had been imprisoned for civil disobedience. Using such tactics as disrupting corporate board meetings, his followers had pushed for higher wages and job training. Hillary interviewed Alinsky, now an elderly man, in Chicago and got him to speak at Wellesley.

Saul Alinsky (third from left) was a major inspiration for Hillary's interests in politics and social activism. (Corbis)

In the spring of 1969, Hillary had to decide what was next after Wellesley. For a while she thought about accepting an opportunity to do social work as a volunteer in India. She also seriously considered an offer from Saul Alinsky, who was willing to pay her as a trainee in his new institute for developing community political activities concerned with consumer protection, the environment, jobs, and the renewal of inner cities.

Another choice was law school. Hillary interviewed at nearby Harvard Law School, where a prominent professor told her, "We don't need any more women." She applied to Yale Law School in New Haven, Connecticut, and was accepted as one of 30 women among 140 freshmen. She decided to attend Yale after leaving Wellesley.

A Standing Ovation

Hillary and her classmates learned that at the June 1969 graduation ceremonies, the Wellesley trustees planned to give an honorary degree to Massachusetts senator Edward Brooke, a formerly liberal Republican who had become a supporter of Richard Nixon. Some seniors wanted to stage a counter-commencement of their own. Several, including Hillary, went to Wellesley president Ruth Adams to propose that commencement exercises include a student speaker.

Adams said no. Wellesley, she pointed out, had never done that. The students, without Hillary, tried again, recommending Hillary because she was president of student government. Adams gave in, agreeing only after Hillary promised to let her review her remarks in advance.

With only three days to go, Hillary and her friends hastily drafted a text. Adams approved. Senator Brooke spoke at commencement. He talked broadly of the student protest movement as "healthy self-criticism" but condemned the SDS, implying it had given aid and comfort to Vietnamese leader Ho Chi Min.

Then Hillary stepped up to the podium. She set aside her prepared remarks. Without notes, she scolded the senator, accusing him of using insulting rhetoric to defend Nixon. "Every protest, every dissent," she said, "is unabashedly an attempt to forge an identity in this particular age. That for many of us over the past four years has meant coming to terms with our humanness."

Noting that the senator had expressed "empathy" with student complaints, Hillary said, "Empathy doesn't do anything. We've had lots of empathy, but for too long our leaders have used politics as the art of the possible. The challenge now is to practice making what appears to be impossible, possible."

Although some parents and older alumnae found the remarks rude, most of the crowd rose to its feet in a standing ovation that lasted seven minutes. That evening, just to prove she could rebel in more ways than one, Hillary went for a swim where swimming was never allowed, in the college's Lake Waban. While she swam, a campus guard seized her glasses and street clothes. In her wet bathing suit, the near-sighted new graduate had to find her way home to her dorm.

Hillary delivers her memorable speech at the Wellesley College commencement ceremony, 1969. (Wellesley College Archives)

That year, *LIFE* magazine ran a picture of Wellesley commencement speaker Hillary Rodham, citing her as one of the three best and brightest student activists in the nation.

3

GIRL MEETS BOY

When Hillary arrived at Yale Law School in the fall of 1969, the campus and the city of New Haven were receiving national attention. That August, Bobby Seale, the leader of an African-American group called the Black Panthers, had been indicted along with eight other Panthers (the media referred to them as the "Black Panther Nine") for the New Haven murder of a member whom they had suspected of being a police informant. As prosecution and defense lawyers prepared for the trial scheduled for May, outrage mounted against the New Haven police.

One of Hillary's professors, Professor Thomas Emerson, specialized in trial proceedings related to the U.S. Constitution's First Amendment. He assigned Hillary and others to attend the trial and to watch for civil rights abuses by the prosecutors. She took charge of setting up a schedule, ensuring that at least one Yale Law student was always present in the courtroom. She worked closely with the Panthers' lead attorney, Charles Garry, and helped deliver regular reports on student findings to Panther headquarters.

Hillary was one of many who were ready for a violent protest because of the trials. She saw Yale dorms thrown open to demonstrators and city businesses closed with plywood nailed over windows. She knew of fire-bombings at the nearby Wesleyan College campus, of blasting caps stolen from a Yale chemistry lab, of "Burn Yale" signs carried amidst a crowd of some 15,000 students from Yale and other schools. Through the intense days of the trial, Hillary's skills at presiding over meetings kept them from becoming chaotic shouting matches. She insisted on maintaining open lines of communication with the college administration. Her friends saw her work hard to calm many upset students.

Children and the Law

Amid the furor over the Panthers trial, Hillary met a Yale Law graduate, Marian Wright Edelman, who was a visiting lecturer that spring and delivered a speech entitled "Children and the Law." The daughter of a Baptist minister in South Carolina, Edelman had been the first African-American admitted to the bar in Mississippi. She and her husband, Peter Edelman, who had served as Senator Robert Kennedy's legislative assistant, had been active in the civil rights movement and in administering the programs of Johnson's Great Society. That experience had taught them that while most Americans were not eager to bestow welfare on adults, almost no one could deny the need to help children.

The message in Edelman's Yale speech was that as a society we owe the gift of welfare to all children who need it. Law student Hillary Rodham was so impressed that she immediately asked the visiting speaker for a chance to work during the summer in her Washington Research Project (later to be renamed the Children's Defense Fund). Since Edelman's budget had no room for such an internship, Hillary, on her own, obtained a grant to cover her expenses. She spent the summer on the staff of Senator Walter Mondale of Minnesota, who chaired a subcommittee studying the living conditions of migrant workers and their children in labor camps.

Hillary's experience that summer set her on a new path. Starting her second year of law school, she took courses in the Yale Child Study Center, combining legal studies with child psychology. Doing research on disputes over the custody of children, she helped the authors of a book on the subject. She also assisted a Legal Aid lawyer

Marion Wright Edelman and Hillary Rodham Clinton, 2003
(Associated Press)

who defended penniless children and their parents against the harsh, unsympathetic custody rulings of state welfare authorities. (The Legal Aid Society is a law firm that provides volunteer legal services for people who cannot afford lawyers.) This gave Hillary firsthand experience in family law.

That fall, Hillary was invited to join the editorial board of the *Yale Review*, a radical law magazine founded only the year before to compete with the staid and traditional *Yale Law Journal*.

"We might as well introduce ourselves."

One day late in the fall of 1970, Hillary was studying in the law school library. From her seat far back in the long, narrow room, she noticed a tall, heavyset man looking at her from just inside the entrance. He wore a full beard, and he more than needed a haircut. After a few minutes, she got up and walked toward him. "Look," she said, "if you're going to keep staring at me and I'm going to keep staring back, we might as well introduce ourselves."

The man was Bill Clinton. A first-year law student from Arkansas, Clinton's first political role was president of his junior class in high school. On a Washington, D.C., trip as a senator in American Legion Boys Nation—a program that annually sends two boys from each state to the capital for a week to learn how bills move through the U.S. Senate—he had shaken President Kennedy's hand in the White House Rose Garden. He had been president of his freshman class at Georgetown University and had served as an intern in the office of J. William Fulbright, an Arkansas senator and chairman of the Senate Foreign Relations Committee. Clinton had then won a prestigious Rhodes Scholarship and spent two years at Oxford, England's oldest university. Now he was in New Haven because he intended to run for public office, and a Yale law degree was known to be a strong key to a political career.

Hillary's friends could see that it was love at first sight. Bill's friends watched the couple strolling on the campus and said they were obviously in love, despite their many differences. Bill was an extrovert who had long ago lost count of girlfriends. Hillary was, despite her reputation as a hard-nosed liberal leader, a shy, somewhat over-weight woman who wore ragged jeans and big, thick eye-glasses. "She was like a den mother to all the guys," said one classmate.

Hillary attended classes, made notes, read her assign-ments, and was always on time. Bill skipped many classes, borrowed other students' notes, was always read-ing something that had not been assigned, and was usu-ally late. Friends who could see how these opposites attracted each other also noticed that, when it came to marks, each got an A.

In the summer of 1971, Hillary took an internship in the Oakland, California, law office of Robert Treuhaft, a former communist whom she had met when he helped Charles Garry defend the Black Panther Nine. When she returned to Connecticut, she and Bill moved into a small one-bedroom apartment near the Yale campus. Since she was one year ahead of Bill at Yale, she decided to put off graduating from law school in June 1972 so she could take more courses at the Child Study Center and graduate with Bill in 1973.

During this time, Hillary was becoming more and more devoted to the rights of children. Her friend Marian Edelman helped her get a job as research assistant with the Carnegie Council on Children, a group of 11 experts who were producing a book-length report titled *All Our Children*. Their thesis was that government should not only be responsible for children's educations (as it had been for well over a century) but that it should also pay for childhood disability insurance, child care, family leave, universal health care, supplemental income for poor families, and full employment for one or both parents, even if it meant that government had to create the jobs. The report also promoted laws to keep schools from expelling or suspending students who were disruptive and to permit children to confer with doctors about pregnancy or drug use without informing their parents.

First Political Appearance

In May 1972, with its national presidential convention scheduled for Miami Beach that summer, the Democratic National Committee's platform committee was holding a regional meeting in Boston's Faneuil Hall. The platform committee was responsible for declaring the party's policies and principles. Marian Wright Edelman, who presided over the session, invited Hillary to be one of some 50 speakers, including the mayors of Boston and

Providence, Rhode Island. The *New York Times* reported, "Hillary Rodham of the Yale Law School said the party must respond to a growing movement to extend civil and political rights to children."

That summer, Hillary and Bill worked for the presidential campaign of Democratic candidate George McGovern. Bill helped manage the Texas operation (where there was little hope of winning), and Hillary ran a San Antonio drive to register voters.

The following spring, in 1973, Hillary went with Bill to Arkansas, where they each took the state's bar exam.

4

AN ARKANSAS LAWYER

After graduating from law school, Hillary and Bill split up for a time. He went to teach at the University of Arkansas Law School in Fayetteville, a job sure to open the door to a career in Arkansas politics. She went to Cambridge, Massachusetts, to work at the Children's Defense Fund office.

Within six months Hillary received a call from Yale Law professor Burke Marshall, who had admired Hillary's career in New Haven. Marshall said that a lawyer named John Doar was heading the legal staff of the House of Representatives' Judiciary Committee, which was looking into impeaching President Richard Nixon over his handling of the burglary of Democratic Party headquarters in the Watergate Hotel. Marshall asked Hillary to join Doar's staff. She accepted, thereby becoming part of one of the most prominent legal investigations in U.S. history.

Planning an Impeachment

By January, Hillary was in Washington, D.C., working from dawn to late at night seven days a week in a crowded, stuffy office. As one of three women among the 43 staff lawyers, she was assigned to draft rules for the presentation of evidence. She also helped compile a book-length report on the history of abuses of power by presidents. The report, titled *Responses of the Presidents to Charges of Misconduct*, was kept secret until after Nixon resigned. Using the controversial Oval Office audio tapes, she helped to analyze the process of decision-making within the Nixon White House and track the cover-up to Nixon's desk.

John Doar liked Hillary. She was one of the few assistants he included in the confidential executive meetings of the Judiciary Committee as he argued for the impeachment of the president on three charges: obstruction of justice, abuse of power, and contempt of Congress.

Throughout the investigation, committee staff lawyers were expected to keep their personal opinions to themselves. Hillary, however, let her dislike of Nixon be known, arguing that the president should be impeached not only for his Watergate behavior but for ordering the secret bombing of Vietcong supply lines in Cambodia, a country against which the U.S. had not declared war.

On July 24, 1974, the U.S. Supreme Court ruled that Nixon had to release the Oval Office tapes that proved his involvement in the attempt to cover up the burglary. The Judiciary Committee then voted the three articles of impeachment. On August 9, rather than face trial in the Senate, Nixon became the first U.S. president to resign from office.

With the work of the committee now finished, Hillary packed up to leave Washington, D.C. She left behind many new friends to whom she had mentioned her boyfriend in Arkansas who, she insisted, would some day be president.

The Hippie Girlfriend

Hillary headed for Arkansas and a job teaching at the law school where Bill worked. He was not only teaching law; he was running for a seat in the U.S. House of Representatives. She settled in at his campaign headquarters and set about shaping up his not always dependable volunteers. Her job was not easy. Wearing her baggy dress and sandals in a land where beauty-parlor hairdos and makeup counted, she was considered "the hippie girlfriend." But she soon earned the workers' respect when they saw and heard her advise her boyfriend on how to conduct interviews and press conferences.

Her real test came on election day 1974, when she learned that one of Bill's campaign workers—doing "what everybody does"—had $15,000 cash in hand ready to pay off some poll workers for fixing the vote count. Hillary stopped him. Committing election fraud, she said, was not the route to Congress.

Clinton's opponent won the election. But Arkansas politicians began calling Bill the Boy Wonder, and Democrats nationwide took notice.

A Cozy House on California Street

Hillary and Bill continued teaching law. He was the popular professor who gave easy marks, was slow to grade papers, and schmoozed in the lounge with his students. She was tough, demanding punctual, organized work and excusing no one. She not only taught but found time to start the university's first legal-aid clinic, which offered services similar to those of the Legal Aid Society. In its first year, the legal-aid clinic advised some 300 clients and handled 50 cases in court.

Over the next year, Hillary held off against marriage proposals from Bill. While she knew she loved him, she was not convinced that a future in Arkansas was right for her. Since Bill had lost the race for Congress, living in Washington—where she had friends and connections from her experience with the Judiciary Committee—was out of the question, and he was now talking of running for state attorney general and later for governor. But in Arkansas, they both knew, a man who lived with a woman who was not his wife had little chance of election to such offices.

In the summer of 1975, Hillary scheduled a vacation trip to visit friends up north. As Bill was driving her to the airport, they passed a small house with a for-sale sign on California Street in Fayetteville. Hillary said it looked cozy.

When she returned, Bill met her plane, then stopped in front of that house and told her he had bought it. "Now you'd better marry me," he said, "because I can't live there all by myself."

Hillary said yes. They were married on October 11, 1975. But Hillary Rodham said that her name, both professional and private, would remain Hillary Rodham.

The Rose Law Firm

In winning the primary race that gave him the Democratic nomination for Attorney General of Arkansas, Bill Clinton showed such zeal that the Republicans nominated no one to run against him in the general election. He spent the fall of 1976 serving as Arkansas chairman of Jimmy Carter's campaign for the U.S. presidency, while Hillary was in Indiana as deputy coordinator for Carter's field operations.

They sold the California Street house and bought a small brick house in Little Rock. With Bill earning only $6,000 a year as state attorney general in Little Rock, Hillary needed a job. A lawyer named Vincent Foster, who admired Hillary's work with the university's legal services clinic, recommended her to his firm, Rose, Nash, Williamson, Carroll, Clay and Giroir—known as the Rose Law Firm.

As a first-year associate, Hillary was the Rose firm's first female lawyer, its first northern feminist, and its first politician's wife. She quickly earned a reputation not only for her exceptional brains and strong opinions but for not wearing makeup and for dieting on lettuce from a plastic bag at her desk.

During this time she contributed a chapter to *Children's Rights: Contemporary Perspectives*, a book by Patricia Vadin and Ilene Brody. In it she urged those working on behalf of children to sue the makers of junk food and the builders of nuclear power plants to prevent them from harming children.

During that first year she also lobbied for improvements in the Arkansas child welfare system and helped found Arkansas Advocates for Children and Families, which in turn created the Governor's Commission on Early Childhood. It provided new state money for child-care programs.

Webb Hubbell, a Rose partner, was impressed with first-year associate Hillary Rodham's independence and idealism. He helped her become counsel for the Little Rock Airport Commission, a position that put her in touch with powerful local officials.

In December 1977, President Jimmy Carter appointed Hillary to the board of the Legal Services Corporation (LSC), a group of lawyers responsible for the distribution of government money to local legal-aid programs nationwide. The board shortly elected her chairman, putting her, at the age of 30, in charge of a multi-million-dollar national organization. Started under President Johnson's Great Society program, the LSC had been made an independent corporation by an act of Congress in 1974. When Hillary took charge, the LSC's budget was well over $100 million, and it was making grants in nearly every county in every state and territory of the U.S. In Hillary's opinion, its purpose was not merely to provide low-income people with standard legal services. Rather, the LSC had the power, through the justice system, to redistribute wealth to the poor.

Her work with the LSC took Hillary back and forth to Washington, New York, and other cities. In the meantime her husband, now the Arkansas attorney general, was a well-known Little Rock political figure, but one whose list of girlfriends kept growing—even after he and Hillary were married.

5

FIRST LADY OF ARKANSAS

Two important events happened to Hillary and Bill in the summer of 1978. One was that Bill, as attorney general in office, entered the primary election and won the Democratic nomination to run for governor. The other was that friends Jim and Susan McDougal offered Bill and Hillary a half interest in a 230-acre property they were developing on the scenic White River in northwest Arkansas. On it, they planned to create vacation and retirement homes. The McDougals had already obtained a $182,611 mortgage loan from a bank, so Hillary and Bill didn't have to invest any money. Bill and Hillary co-signed the mortgage note, which meant they could be responsible for repaying the entire amount. They were now co-owners of the Whitewater Development Company.

A third important event came on October 11, when Hillary deposited $6,000 with a stock-brokerage firm to open a commodities-trading account. Commodities are physical goods such as basic foods (for example, sugar, corn, oats, and peanuts) and raw materials (for example, crude oil, tin, and lead). Traders in commodities buy and sell the actual commodities or buy and sell contracts for the future deliveries of commodities. Trading in commodities futures is a high-risk gamble, because no one can guarantee what a future price may be. Hillary traded in cattle futures. By December 11, two months after she started trading, her commodities contracts were worth $2,300,000.

Into the Governor's Mansion

In January 1979, Bill Clinton was inaugurated governor of Arkansas. When Hillary moved with her husband into the governor's mansion in Little Rock, she was 31 and he was 32—the youngest governor in the U.S. since 1938 (when Minnesota's Harold Stassen took office at age 31). In one interview, Hillary remarked that she would not be using Clinton as a last name because, "I need to maintain my interests and my commitments. I need my own identity, too." To help prove that point, Hillary dismissed her offi-cial Arkansas state police escort and drove her own car.

Hillary was busy. The Rose law firm had made her its first woman partner. That meant she was expected to attract clients to the firm. Being first lady included presid-ing at official Arkansas State events and making speeches around the state. Appointed by the governor, she headed a committee to advise on health care needs in rural areas. Her duties as chairman of the Legal Services Corporation took her frequently to Washington, D.C., and New York.

Hillary spent much of the spring helping organize a pet project, the Governor's School. Held on a college campus, the summer-school program was much like the University of Life that the Reverend Don Jones had introduced to Hillary and her teenage group. It gave 400 gifted high school juniors six weeks of academic courses as well as open discussions described as "critical thinking" and "feelings." It became an annual event.

A Daughter Named Chelsea

In the summer of 1979, Hillary realized that she was expecting a baby. With that news, she closed her commodities-trading account, saying she didn't want investment risks giving her emotional pressure while she was pregnant.

Chelsea Clinton, named for a song by the artist Joni Mitchell, was born February 27, 1980. Her 32-year-old mother took four months' maternity leave from the Rose firm, then worked part time for another two months. By summer of that year, she and Bill were busy getting ready for an election campaign, as at the time the Arkansas governor's term was only two years.

Cheslea Clinton and Hillary in Peking, China, 1998
(Associated Press)

Makeover

Bill's Republican opponent, Frank White, found an issue to pound on during the election. In political ads, he demanded to know why the governor's wife was called Ms. Rodham and not Mrs. Clinton. Married women in Arkansas all took their husbands' names, he pointed out, so why didn't she?

White won the election. Hillary immediately went to work organizing a comeback for Bill. She sent for Dick

Morris, a well-known expert at taking polls. He soon had survey results that indicated what Arkansas voters were thinking. It was time, he said, for Hillary to have a makeover. Her frizzy hairdo, flowery loose-fitting dresses, and thick eyeglasses, he said, had to go. And, he added, she and Bill had better start showing up at church on Sunday mornings.

Hillary took the advice. She even forced herself, despite the discomfort, to wear contact lenses. She regularly attended the congregation at the First Methodist Church, while Bill sang in the choir at Immanuel Baptist. Perhaps the most difficult part of the makeover, from Hillary's point of view, came on February 27, 1982—Chelsea's second birthday—when Bill announced his candidacy for a second nomination for the governorship: The press was told that "Mrs. Clinton" would take leave from the Rose firm to campaign with her husband.

Hillary's makeover seemed to help Bill's campaign for a return to the governor's mansion. The *Arkansas Gazette* told its readers before election day:

> Mrs. Clinton is almost certainly the best speaker among politicians' wives. She is an Illinois native, perhaps a little brisker, a little more outspoken than the traditional Southern governor's lady. The name change indicates that she's working at softening her image a bit and succeeding, apparently. She has become a good handshaking campaigner in the traditional Arkansas style.

The fact that she has become accomplished at what is a rather passive role for a person of her background and temperament probably is a tribute to self-discipline. Her spirit shows when she speaks on her husband's behalf.

Back at Home in the Governor's Mansion

In January 1983, Governor and Mrs. Clinton moved back to the governor's mansion in Little Rock. Democratic president Jimmy Carter moved out of the White House, and Republican Ronald Reagan moved in. The change of administration ended Hillary's term as chairman of the board of the LSC, which then had an annual budget of more than $300 million. She joined the board of the New World Foundation (NWF), a philanthropic organization that gave grants to such liberal groups as the Children's Defense Fund, on which she was also a board member.

During his second term, Governor Bill Clinton soon saw a chance to improve Arkansas public education. The Arkansas Supreme Court ruled that the way in which state money was dispensed to public schools was discriminatory: Rich school districts were treated better than poor districts. Governor Clinton asked the Arkansas State board of education to appoint a commission to determine how to fix the problem. Hillary volunteered to head the commission.

Over the summer of 1983, Hillary took another leave of absence from the Rose firm and held hearings in each of the state's 75 counties. In public speeches statewide, she let Arkansans know that out of 370 school districts, 91 high schools taught no chemistry, more than 100 had no mathematics curricula, and roughly half taught neither a foreign language nor physics. No wonder, she said, that standardized tests were bewildering to Arkansas high school students. It was also no wonder that Arkansas stood last among the 50 states in the number of high school graduates going to college.

"Life goes on after seventeen."

Statewide, Arkansans began to admire Hillary for her courage in telling them, "The first purpose of school is to educate, not to provide entertainment or opportunities to socialize. Discipline holds no mystery. When it is firm, clearly understood, fairly administered and perceived to be so, it works. When it isn't, it doesn't."

A small-town audience where the high school football or basketball game was the event of the week had to nod in agreement when Hillary told them bluntly that a reading teacher was as important to their children as a football or basketball coach. "This isn't only for the benefit of the students who don't participate in sports and cheerleading," she said, "but it's also for the benefit of those who do participate because high school activities don't last forever and life goes on after seventeen."

In the fall of 1983, the 15-person commission led by Hillary presented its recommendations: limits on class size, a lengthened school year, no high school diploma without 13 1/2 units of academic courses, mandatory kindergarten in all school districts, one guidance counselor for every 600 high school students and every 450 elementary students, 70 percent of all school budgets to be spent on salaries, and no promotion to fourth, seventh, or ninth grade until the student passed a standardized test.

Getting the changes made was not easy. The governor had to ask the state legislature for tax increases to pay for the education improvements. The only one the legislators approved was a one-cent rise in the state's sales tax. But they liked Hillary's strong presentation of the education commission's report. "I think," said one, "we've elected the wrong Clinton."

National Acclaim

News of the educational debate in Arkansas helped make Governor and Mrs. Clinton famous nationwide for supporting educational standards. *Esquire* magazine listed each of them among 272 outstanding baby boomers—"the best of the new generation." The National Association of Social Workers made them Public Citizens of the Year. An appearance on television's *Face the Nation* brought Bill

Clinton's face into millions of American living rooms. The Arkansas Press Association named Hillary "Headliner of the Year," the *Arkansas Democrat* saluted her as "Woman of the Year," and the Arkansas Association of American Mothers honored her as "Young Mother of the Year."

With this type of national exposure, Democratic politicians began to think of Hillary's husband as a serious contender for national office. He was a governor who had battled a strong union—the Arkansas teachers—and won. Yet, even though states such as Texas and Georgia enacted competency tests for teachers, not everyone recognized that Hillary had done the grinding work of convincing the Arkansas legislature to accept such tests.

In the fall of 1984, Bill Clinton was re-elected governor. Shortly thereafter, he was elected vice chairman of the National Governors Association, which set up a task force, with Bill as co-chairman, to produce a five-year plan to improve America's schools by establishing national standards for teachers and raising their pay.

At home, Hillary faced family problems. Her husband's half brother, Roger Clinton, was indicted in July 1984 by a federal grand jury for drug trafficking. After pleading guilty, he was sentenced on January 27, 1985, to two to five years in prison. Hillary also became aware that Bill had been seeing a local television reporter named Gennifer Flowers, as well as other girlfriends.

6

MOVING INTO NATIONAL POLITICS

By summer of 1985, Hillary was letting old friends up north know that she was considering divorce. But then she began to think things over. Her husband was running for another two-year term as governor. He was being recognized nationally. And she had earned a name for herself—a name associated with her husband's—as a person who got things done. Hillary decided that the most important thing was to help Bill Clinton become what she had long ago said he would become: the president of the United States.

At the Rose law firm in April 1985, Hillary had accepted Jim McDougal as a client. (McDougal and his wife had brought the Clintons into the Whitewater Development Company in 1978.) He was running the Madison Guaranty

Savings & Loan bank, which was in poor financial condition and facing threats from the Federal Home Loan Bank Board to shut it down. Bank examiners suspected that McDougal was running a scam by making fraudulent real-estate deals and false loans to friends and relatives while the money was actually going into his pocket.

The federal bank board ordered McDougal to raise more capital if he wanted Madison Guaranty to stay in business. McDougal proposed selling preferred stock to investors. (Investors who own preferred stock have an advantage: They are paid dividends before those who invest in common stock are paid.) This plan had to be approved by the Arkansas Securities Commission. In a telephone call, Hillary convinced the state commissioner of securities to approve Madison Guaranty's stock sale. No stock was issued, however, because the bank soon fell apart financially.

A month later, in May, McDougal was selling off Whitewater lots to raise cash. He proposed that Hillary and Bill sign over their half interest to him and his wife, Susan, letting them become responsible for Whitewater's mounting debts. Bill agreed. Susan took a stock certificate to the Rose firm for Hillary to sign. Hillary refused.

"Jim told me," she said, "that this was going to pay for college for Chelsea. I still expect it to do that."

In November 1986, Arkansas voters gave Bill Clinton his fourth term in office. They also approved changing their state's constitution to make the term four years. *Newsweek* magazine immediately declared Clinton a candidate for president in 1988.

Putting off a Run for the Presidency

In the spring of 1987, with the convention to nominate a presidential candidate just a year away, Arkansas governor Bill Clinton made speeches to Democratic Party groups in 18 different states. In March he was in California for a Hollywood dinner at which producer Norman Lear introduced him to major party contributors. In April he spoke to New Hampshire Democrats, whose support is always a key early step toward nomination. In May, Gary Hart, the Democrat who was considered the front-runner, dropped out of the race after the news media disclosed that he (a married man) had been conducting an affair with a young woman named Donna Rice.

Hart's departure made Hillary's husband the front-runner. Hillary's parents sold their suburban Chicago home and bought a Little Rock condo so they could take care of seven-year-old Chelsea while Hillary and Bill hit the campaign trail. The press was notified that on July 15, at the Excelsior Hotel in Little Rock, the governor would formally announce his candidacy.

Before July 15, however, close friends of Hillary and the governor confronted Bill. The revelation of facts about

Hart's private life, they pointed out, had proved that a leading candidate for the nation's top office could not have a private life. And a long list of candidate Bill Clinton's girlfriends, whether or not Hillary knew about any or all of them, was just what reporters and columnists would love to get.

At the hotel on July 15, Bill announced that he was not running. A presidential campaign, he said, would take too much of his time away from Chelsea. Hillary stood on the sidelines—angry, according to some witnesses, and eyes in tears, according to others.

Friends saw this as a moment of crisis in the Clintons' lives. Some said that only now did Hillary admit knowing about her husband's long string of girlfriends. Others said she was stymied by the idea that she would be the family breadwinner and a resident of the governor's mansion in Little Rock for years to come. Still others were sure that Hillary thought about divorce but stuck with Bill because of Chelsea.

Bill soon declared his support for the nomination of Massachusetts governor Michael Dukakis. He then gave the nominating speech at the Atlanta convention. Bill's speech was a disaster. With the auditorium's lights failing to dim and thus quiet the boisterous crowd, the talk's 32 minutes seemed endless. Yet, in a reverse negative way, the long speech helped to spread his fame.

Corporate Boards, Gender and Race Bias, and Children's Defense

Back at the Rose firm, Hillary had a busy 1987. In a rough game of office politics, she, Webb Hubbell, and Vince Foster teamed up to force the replacement of the firm's chairman. She herself was invited to accept positions on the boards of directors of such major Arkansas corporations as Tyson Foods and Wal-Mart. She was now making about $100,000 a year but was so busy with activities outside the office (including her official duties as first lady of Arkansas) that she earned only about one third the pay of other Rose partners.

In one of those outside activities, Hillary accepted in 1987 the chairmanship of a special commission of the American Bar Association (ABA). Its goal was "to promote equal participation of women and minorities in the legal profession." Over the next four years, the commission held many public hearings and created manuals for ABA members on such subjects as day care, parental leave, and sexual harassment. To help fight discrimination against women and minorities in local bar associations as well as federal and state courts nationwide, Hillary's commission established "gender and race bias task forces." They worked to get women and minorities promoted as judges and as senior partners in law firms as well as to include more women and minorities on juries hearing cases involving harassment and discrimination.

Hillary was also chairman of the Children's Defense Fund. In 1989 it fought a proposal from the first Bush administration to let parents use tax credits to pay for whatever day care they chose for their children. The Children's Defense Fund proposed a bill in Congress called the Act for Better Children (ABC). Spending $2.5 billion in its first year, it would impose federal regulations on day-care centers.

Hillary knew that after World War II the French had established day care as a responsibility of government. She led a 14-member study group to France for a two-week visit to day-care facilities. As expected, the group found the closely regulated French system superior to America's day-care system. In an article in the *New York Times*, Hillary said that Americans assume "that parents alone can always determine and then provide—personally or through the marketplace—what's best for their children and, hence, society. To do our children justice, we need to develop a nationwide consensus on how to best nurture our children."

Although Congress did not enact the ABC bill, this was just another example of Hillary's commitment to improving the lives of children through new legislation.

The Right Time to Run

The fall of 1990 brought Bill's re-election for his fifth term as Arkansas governor. He had promised voters he would not run for president, but by spring he was criss-crossing the U.S. to make speeches and meet Democratic leaders. Hillary sensed that the timing was right for Bill to try for the White House. The Republicans had occupied it for almost 12 years, and voters might well be ready for a change. The Persian Gulf War in February 1991 had brought George Herbert Walker Bush one of the highest approval ratings in presidential history, but already his rating was dropping along with the economy. Among Bill's supporters, Hillary spread the idea that the amiable young Southern governor could be elected president of the United States.

By summertime, Hillary had enlisted an old friend, Mickey Kantor, with whom she had served on the board of the LSC, to organize a national campaign.

7

TOWARD THE WHITE HOUSE

On October 3, 1991, Bill Clinton stood on the steps of Little Rock's Old State House and announced his candidacy for the Democratic nomination for President. Many who had known Hillary and Bill for a long time thought it was a moment she had dreamed of as far back as Yale Law School. At least one member of the Children's Defense Fund board had recently heard her say, "Well, Bill and I are going to run," and most of their friends knew that Hillary's strong opinions and ability to make hard decisions were a major force behind Bill's career. Now she set to work organizing finances and fund-raising, renting office space, pulling together committees and chairpersons, and filing the papers needed to enter the primary elections in New Hampshire and Texas.

Together on *60 Minutes*

Amid the flurry of news announcements and planning came another kind of news. Only six days after Bill's October 3 announcement, a decision by the State Grievance Committee supported an Arkansas government employee who had complained that, while her name was at the top of the list for a promotion, the job she expected had been given to a newer employee named Gennifer Flowers.

The story got the attention of tabloid newspapers. A reporter from one—the weekly *Star*—let Flowers know that he knew not only that Governor Clinton had arranged for her to be hired but that she had been the governor's mistress for some 12 years. Convinced that her story was going to come out, Flowers agreed to sell it to the *Star* and also provided audio tapes she had made of phone calls with Clinton.

By now, Hillary knew the facts. She wanted the world to know she supported Bill, despite his infidelities. At her suggestion, the television program *60 Minutes* arranged for her and Bill to be interviewed on a special edition that would be broadcast immediately after the 1992 Super Bowl.

Interviewer Steve Kroft asked many tough questions about Bill's relationship with Gennifer Flowers. Bill admitted "wrongdoing" and "causing pain in my marriage."

"You've said that your marriage has had problems," said Kroft. "What does that mean? Does it mean adultery? People are sitting out there—the voters—and they're saying, 'Look, it's really pretty simple. If he's never had an extramarital affair why doesn't he say so?'"

Hillary had let Bill do most of the talking. Now she interrupted. "There isn't a person watching this," she said, "who would feel comfortable sitting here on this couch detailing everything that ever went on in life or their marriage. And I think it's real dangerous in this country if we don't have some zone of privacy for everyone."

Moments later, visibly annoyed by Kroft's persistence, Hillary said, "You know, I'm not sitting here—some little woman standing by my man like Tammy Wynette. I'm sitting here because I love him, and I honor what we've been through together. And you know, if that's not enough for people, then heck, don't vote for him."

60 Minutes made Hillary as prominent as her husband, but as she was criticized for misinterpreting the meaning of the song "Stand by Your Man," she later apologized for the Tammy Wynette remark.

"Two for one"

Next came the primary campaigns. Just before the New York State primary in early March, the *New York Times* ran a story on the Whitewater Development Company. It asked whether the Morgan Guaranty Savings & Loan (Jim McDougal's bank), whose failure had cost American taxpayers millions of dollars, had in effect paid for the failure of the Whitewater real estate investment. It also questioned tax deductions related to Whitewater that the Clintons had taken.

Late in March, California governor Jerry Brown, himself a Democratic candidate for president, charged that Hillary's work as a lawyer for Morgan Guaranty was a conflict of interest: Banks were regulated by the state, and she was the wife of the state's governor. When a reporter questioned Hillary, she replied, "I suppose I could have stayed home, baked cookies and had teas, but what I decided was to fulfill my profession, which I entered before my husband was in public life. My gosh, you can't be a lawyer if you don't represent banks."

When Bill's nomination was secured by his winning the Illinois primary, the news media recognized Hillary's role in the victory. "Hillary Clinton may be the candidate's top asset," said the *Chicago Tribune*. "Partner as Much as Wife" was a *Time* magazine headline. "She's an accomplished professional," announced *Newsweek*, "with perhaps as much claim as her husband to a place in public life."

Bill himself backed that idea. "If I get elected," he said in a speech, "we'll do things together." He began using the phrase "Hillary and I" regularly and was eager to point out that the first lady of Arkansas had studied problems and recommended solutions in such fields as child care, health, and education.

At one point, Bill put the hint of a co-presidency into a campaign slogan: "Two for one—buy one, get one free." Hillary confirmed the notion during a speech, saying, "If you vote for my husband, you get me. It's a two-for-one, blue-plate special."

Cookies and Tea

Hillary's remark that "I suppose I could have stayed home, baked cookies and had teas" became a highlight of news reports and talk shows. As the Democrats met in New York City for their convention in July, the *New York Times* featured her favorite cookie recipe in a story that pictured her having tea and cookies with Tipper Gore (wife of future vice president Al Gore) at the Waldorf-Astoria Hotel. During convention week, she gave thousands of cookies to the various delegations from across the state and asked them to vote for her recipe in a bakeoff contest that *Family Circle* magazine was holding. (Hillary's later won, beating a Barbara Bush recipe.)

By now, Hillary's appearance had changed. Her hair had become blonde. Her weight was down. Her wardrobe featured bright pastels rather than drab knit suits. But more than her look had changed. Hillary had also taken a less visible role in the campaign process. The *New York Times* described the difference: "Although Mrs. Clinton was originally seen as a formidable campaigner and hailed as a model new woman, able to balance her family life with a thriving law practice, by early summer she had retreated to the sidelines, appearing publicly only as a quiet presence at her husband's side."

The change was noted on the West Coast, too. The *Los Angeles Times* reported: "Hillary Clinton's campaign to get her husband of sixteen years elected has taken an unacknowledged midcourse change in emphasis, to put forward the kinder, gentler Hillary Clinton, to round off some of the sharper edges, to convince voters that she is not an ambitious, hectoring manipulator but one more working mom juggling through hectic days—a new American traditionalist, as down-home likable as she is intellectually admirable."

On November 3, 1992, Bill Clinton was elected the 42d president of the United States. Winning 43 percent of the vote, he beat both incumbent Republican president George Herbert Walker Bush and Reform party candidate Ross Perot.

As the country waited for Inauguration Day, it wondered how strong a voice the new first lady would have in the White House. Some people began guessing. They noticed, for example, that Hillary showed up unexpectedly at Bill's first working dinner with Democratic leaders in Congress. "She knows more about this stuff," explained the president-elect, "than most of us do."

A reporter asked one of Bill's aides if Mrs. Clinton would attend meetings of the president's cabinet. "Cabinet meetings," came the reply, "would be a step down for her." And another aide told a *U.S. News & World Report* journalist, "Of course she's in the loop. She is the loop."

A FIRST LADY IN CHARGE

About ten weeks pass between a president's election and inauguration on January 20. That time is called the transition period. The transition from the Bush administration to the Clinton administration was like no other in U.S. history, for the woman who was to be first lady took a much larger role in the transition than any of her predecessors had.

Friends in High Places

In more ways than anyone could measure, Hillary had been responsible for Bill Clinton's nomination and election. She also determined many, if not most, appointments to the Clinton cabinet and to White House staff positions. Some appointees were friends with whom Hillary and Bill had worked or who dated back to college and law school days. In the Justice Department, Webb Hubbell from the Rose firm was named associate attorney general, while Hillary's Wellesley classmate Eleanor Acheson got the job of recommending candidates for federal judgeships. Others who had been Yale professors, Children's Defense Fund fund-raisers or board members, or longtime friends were appointed to key positions.

The two most influential White House jobs are chief of staff and White House counsel. Hillary urged Bill to appoint his childhood friend Mack McLarty as chief of staff. In this role, McLarty would be responsible for keeping the Oval Office functioning as efficiently as possible under a president who was already famous for ignoring schedules and making up his timetable as he went along.

Hillary asked Bernie Nussbaum to serve as White House counsel. She had kept in touch with him ever since

The presidential inauguration, 1993 (Library of Congress)

they worked together on John Doar's Watergate Judiciary staff. Her close friend Vince Foster, from the Rose firm, took the job of assistant White House counsel.

The White House counsel serves as the lawyer for the presidency. However, the counsel is not the president's personal lawyer. Rather, it protects the office of the nation's chief executive from making legal errors. Its staff checks out every speech the president makes, every proposal for legislation that he sends to Congress, and every bill from Congress or presidential proclamation or executive order that he has to sign. All are reviewed for legal correctness. The counsel office also advises the president on matters of White House policy, taking advantage of loopholes and avoiding potholes. Ethical questions go through the office, too, as do checks on security clearances and statements of financial disclosure.

Although Nussbaum and Foster were officially in charge of this major area, all those moving into White House staff offices knew that Hillary Rodham Clinton was unofficially in charge. More broadly, the only areas of government that she would not be overseeing were foreign affairs and environmental policy.

Task Force on Health Care

The new president had been in office only five days when he announced that Hillary would head his National Task

Force on Health Care Reform. Giving the task force only 100 days to draft a bill to present to Congress, he said his wife was "better at organizing people from a complex beginning to a certain end than anybody I've ever worked with in my life."

Hillary had been thinking about health care throughout her adult life. Now she was the only first lady in U.S. history to hold authority in a government position. She toured the nation making speeches on the need for a health plan, just as she had toured Arkansas marketing her education plan. On Capitol Hill she made dozens of calls on senators and representatives. She welcomed the chance to talk with Washington tourists, special interest groups, and lobbyists for insurance and medical plans.

The plan produced by the task force tried to make all Americans share equally in the cost of health care. It proposed "alliances" run by the governments of the 50 states that would set up contracts with health plans, supervise the collection of insurance premiums, and pay out the benefits. Every family would belong to a health maintenance organization (HMO). Limits would be put on the costs of insurance premiums and on the overall total to be spent yearly on health care, with Medicare payments reduced by $124 billion in the first year. A National Drug Price Advisory Board would determine whether drug prices were fair. A central government file would hold everybody's medical records. The government would determine the courses offered in medical schools.

Many who looked the plan over said that, for the American family, it all added up to less choice, fewer services, and more government supervision. Employers would be required to pay for most of the premiums, with the government paying for people who were not insured. To make sure that individuals and companies conformed to regulations, government agencies and boards made up of political appointees would decide who got what kind of health care at what price.

Hillary took the health care plan to Capitol Hill. Introducing it, she said, "I'm here as a mother, a wife, a daughter, a sister, and a woman." In rapid succession, she presented it to five important committees of the Senate and House of Representatives. Questioned at length, she made it clear that she did not trust the current free-market system of health insurance. "No previous first lady," reported the *New York Times*, "occupied center stage so aggressively or disarmed her critics more effectively."

Despite Hillary's tireless presentation and defense, the Clinton health care plan soon hit two major snags. The first was a money problem. The more benefits the plan promised, the more regulations it would need to run it and the more it would cost—and as the 100 days went by more and more benefits were added. Economists in the new administration couldn't figure out how the national budget could support the plan.

The second snag was even more difficult. From the start, Hillary had insisted that members of her task force operate in secrecy. But the law required that meetings of federal advisory committees be open to the public and that documents of such groups be made public. (A federal advisory committee included such nongovernmental people as representatives of outside groups and interests.) The Association of American Physicians and Surgeons (AAPS), which wanted to preserve private medical practice, filed a request to make public the task force names and working papers.

The White House stonewalled. The AAPS sued. It argued in court that, because Hillary was not a government employee, the task force was an advisory committee. The press and the public, insisted the AAPS, were entitled to attend task force meetings and see working papers and names. Ultimately, U.S. District Judge Royce C. Lamberth ruled that the first lady was not "an employee or even a quasi-employee of the federal government."

The White House appealed. On June 22, the U.S. Court of Appeals (the court that is second only to the Supreme Court of the United States) decided that, for the purposes of the law on advisory committees, Hillary was a federal employee. But it sent the case back to Judge Lamberth,

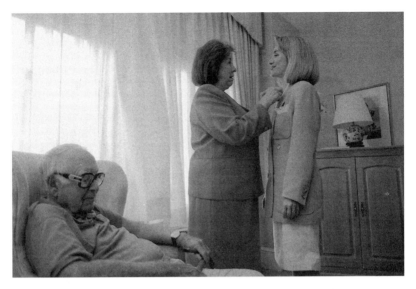

Hillary (far right) with her parents Hugh and Dorothy Rodham in 1992 (Associated Press)

telling him to determine whether task force members worked for the government. After reviewing evidence on 350 people who influenced the task force, the judge announced, "We now know, from records produced in this litigation, that numerous individuals who were never federal employees did much more than just attend working group meetings on an intermittent basis, and we now know that some of these individuals even had supervisory or decision-making roles."

The dispute raged for another three months. The AAPS brought perjury charges against a senior White House adviser, Ira Magaziner, who was supervising the task force.

They challenged a statement he had sworn as true, back in March, that all task force members were government employees. Not until September did the White House, facing the AAPS's lawsuit, agree to make task force names and records open to the public. The AAPS then withdrew their suit.

Busy as she was with the health care task force, in March and April 1993 Hillary had to deal with personal loss. Her 81-year-old father, Hugh Rodham, suffered a stroke and went into a coma. She spent two weeks at his bedside in Little Rock before he died on April 7.

TRAVELGATE AND WHITEWATER

Although health care reform was a prominent political issue early in the Clinton administration, 1993 and 1994 brought controversy to the Clinton White House on several other fronts.

Travelgate

Arranging travel was one of the long-standing functions of the White House's permanent staff. Seven people, including director Billy Dale, who had been on the White House staff for 32 years, worked full time booking flights for staff people, reporters, and camera crews who had to go wherever the president went.

In May 1993, someone discovered that the White House travel office had not been arranging flights for people traveling to and from meetings of the health care task force. Rather, the flights were booked by World Wide Travel, a Little Rock agency the Clinton campaign had used. This led to questions about whether an outside agency could be less costly than the traditional White House travel office. An accounting firm performed an audit of the office and reported that travel office records were not well kept and that $18,000 could not be accounted for.

White House director of administration David Watkins knew that Hillary was furious. "We need to get those people out," he quoted her as saying. "We need our people in." On Wednesday, May 19, 1993, Dale and his staff were replaced, on only 90-minute notice, by employees of World Wide Travel.

That move caused uproar in the press. Commentators nationwide blamed Hillary for the firings and dubbed the event "Travelgate." The reports made such a commotion that two days later the dismissals were revoked, the employees were placed on administrative leave, and the World Wide employees were replaced.

While Hillary now faced what is known as "bad press"— a flood of harsh criticism in newspapers and magazines— the following Sunday, May 23, brought a favorable in-depth profile of her in *The New York Times Sunday Magazine*. The article, titled "Saint Hillary," compared her to American women such as Harriet Beecher Stowe, Carrie Nation, and

Dorothy Day, each of whom had been inspired by her religion to work hard for social improvements.

Vince Foster's Death

Early in July 1993, the president and first lady flew to Japan for an official visit. As Hillary stopped in Little Rock on July 20 on her way back, Mack McLarty, the White House chief of staff, phoned to say that Vince Foster, the assistant White House counsel, had been found dead, apparently of suicide, in Washington's Fort Marcy Park.

Hillary was devastated. Foster had been her best friend at the Rose firm. His strong support had been invaluable through the hectic first six months in the White House. During the dispute over the health care task force, his legal argument had convinced the nation's second-highest court that Hillary was a senior government official. During the travel-office turmoil, he had been a steadying influence. It was he who had called in the accounting firm to look at the facts.

Like any unexpected death, Foster's had to be investigated. He had been taking pills to control depression, but that was not found as the reason for suicide. Some experts said he was overwhelmed by the Travelgate experience and blamed himself for its outcome and for not protecting the first lady from embarrassment. No suicide note was found, and no specific reason for Foster's death was established.

Foster's office was searched carefully, but it took a week before a torn-up note was found in the bottom of his briefcase. Pieced together, it seemed to be a memorandum, or part of a memo, about the travel-office uproar. "No one in the White House, to my knowledge," it said, "violated any law or standard of conduct, including any action in the travel office." The memo went on with comments about the Republicans, the press, and others.

Whitewater

In the fall of 1993, Hillary became aware that the Resolution Trust Corporation (RTC), a federal agency that had investigated a number of failures of savings and loan banks, was checking into Jim and Susan McDougal's records with Morgan Guaranty Savings & Loan. Among witnesses for its inquiry, the RTC named the co-owners of the Whitewater Development Company: Hillary and Bill Clinton.

The *Washington Post* asked the White House to let it see documents of the company that the RTC mentioned. Hillary refused, saying the public was not entitled to know her private financial matters. Her lawyer then arranged for the documents to move to the Justice Department, where the newspapers could not see them.

A Troubled Holiday

While the Whitewater controversy was starting to take shape, the Clintons' first Christmas in Washington was coming. Hillary's mother, Dorothy Rodham, and Bill's mother, Virginia Kelley, and her husband were expected for a visit. Planning had been going on for months, as Christmas at the White House is always conducted on a grand scale.

Hillary invited 70 outstanding American craftspeople to donate their works to a Christmas showcase. Also at her invitation, numbers of crafts groups created angel ornaments—many of them caricatures of her husband. She said they were "funky and down-to-earth."

The family's Christmas spirit was spoiled when, in mid-December, two publications, *The American Spectator* and the *Los Angeles Times*, ran detailed stories on how Arkansas governor Bill Clinton had depended on his state trooper security guards to help him keep dates with girl-friends. In a nation in which the president has no private life, the press and the public were asking how this kind of behavior could be accepted from a man who had to hold the respect of the nation and the world.

Early in the new year, the RTC investigation of Whitewater caught the attention of Congress. The House of Representatives passed a law creating the office of an independent prosecutor—that is, a prosecutor not within the Justice Department. (Such an office had been created during the Watergate investigation in the Nixon administration but had since expired.) The lawyer appointed to the job was a former solicitor general in the recent Bush administration named Kenneth Starr.

Two Press Conferences

The year 1994 began with plenty of controversy for Bill and Hillary Clinton. The *American Spectator* article published in December stated that an Arkansas state clerk named Paula had spent time with Governor Clinton in private. The article implied that they had an intimate relationship. In February 1994, Paula Corbin Jones announced at a press conference that she was suing the president for sexual harassment based on an incident that occurred in 1991.

In March 1994 the *New York Times* published a story on the profits Hillary had made in 1978 when she traded commodities futures. It implied that she had received special treatment because she was the governor's wife. The report brought another storm in the news media as Hillary first said she had made her own trades based on what she knew from *The Wall Street Journal* and then admitted that a lawyer friend had placed trades for her.

Hillary called a televised press conference in the White House's state dining room. For 72 minutes she answered questions about Whitewater—the general heading under which reporters were beginning to put every controversial subject concerning Bill and Hillary Clinton. She said she just didn't know why her trades had been so successful. Asked why she had not paid more attention to how the McDougals were financing the Whitewater mortgage, she said, "Well, shoulda, coulda, woulda, we didn't."

Meanwhile, the first lady's health care plan lingered in Congress until it died there in June 1994. The appeal of the lawsuit by the AAPS ended the following September when the White House released to the AAPS all the documents it wanted.

Inside the White House

During her first 18 months as first lady, Hillary Rodham Clinton set a new and unique tone in the White House. She stayed outside the circle of long-established Washington society, which includes both Democratic and Republican government officials and their spouses. She and Bill welcomed such Hollywood celebrities as Tom Hanks, Barbra Streisand, and Jack Nicholson to movie screenings in the East Wing theater and overnight stays in the Lincoln bedroom.

The Clintons' White House entertaining went on around the clock. In the kitchen, no one was surprised when the first lady sent word, again and again, that large numbers of guests would be arriving for dinner within a couple of hours. The master chef had to cook not only for unpredictable numbers but for a president whose appetite was hearty and a first lady who was serious about dieting.

Then there was what White House memos called the first lady's "no. 1 project." It was a computerized database including some 350,000 people, with Social Security numbers, birth dates, ethnic backgrounds, religions, occupations, positions on policy questions, and other information. Officially identified as WhoDB, it developed from Bill Clinton's own database, which he started in Arkansas in 1982. The supposed purpose of the database was to track official functions, correspondence, and Christmas cards, but reporters learned that it also tracked Democratic donors. Reporters were told it was Hillary's idea. At first she denied this, but later she admitted she started it. "There was no computer system," she said, "and you can't run any modern enterprise without a computer system." Thus, as she had in so many ways throughout her life, Hillary Rodham Clinton was challenging traditions, which in this instance were the ways in which people traditionally thought of the nation's first lady and the White House.

FACING WORLD AUDIENCES AND REPUBLICAN QUESTIONS

In the elections in the autumn of 1994, the Democrats lost majority control in Washington. In both the Senate and the House of Representatives, Republican politicians established special committees—headed by New York senator Alphonse D'Amato and Iowa congressman Jim Leach—to investigate Whitewater. In the House, a Pennsylvania Congressman, William Clinger, was determined to get to the bottom of the Travelgate mystery.

Hillary was familiar with this type of investigation, since she had worked on the Watergate committee planning the impeachment of President Nixon. Thus, she worked with White House lawyers to keep Republican investigators from disclosing various documents to the public. However, some critics said that Hillary's claims of executive privilege—that is, claims that the president was privileged to keep certain matters secret—stretched further than Nixon's claims that Hillary had criticized long ago.

In May 1995 Hillary received a summons to testify before the RTC, which was still investigating Jim McDougal's Madison Guaranty Savings & Loan bank. Documents it had obtained from the Rose firm, said the RTC representatives, did not include billing records on McDougal's Castle Grande Estates project—a trailer park. (A lawyer keeps an hour-by-hour record of time spent working for each client so that the client can be billed for services.) The RTC asked if Hillary had worked on Castle Grande. Under oath, she said no.

Speaking in China

By summer of 1995, Hillary was preparing to go to China. The United Nations' Fourth International Conference on Women was scheduled in Beijing in September. President Clinton named the first lady as honorary chair of the United States delegation, raising hopes worldwide that the U.S. would ratify the UN Convention on the Elimination of Discrimination Against Women (CEDAW), which 143 countries had already endorsed.

*Delivering her acclaimed speech at the Fourth World Confer-
ence on Women in Beijing, China, 1995* (Associated Press)

Thirty-six thousand women attended the conference, most of them representing unofficial nongovernmental organizations. In speeches, workshops, and discussion groups, they talked about a wide variety of women's issues. Hillary Rodham Clinton gave a speech condemning violations of human rights, such as China's forced sterilization of women. "Human rights are women's rights," she said, "and women's rights are human rights." Many considered her speech, which earned countless standing ovations, the high point of the conference.

Before Hillary left for China, Bill had set up the Interagency Council on Women and named Hillary as honorary chair. Its purpose was to get the results of the Beijing meeting into various proposals that the White House would make to the U.S. Congress. Its recommendations ranged from studying the value of "unwaged work"—that is, housework—to eliminating gender biases in education. Once again, Hillary would be playing a prominent role in policy-making during her husband's presidency, which was not common for a U.S. first lady.

It Takes a Village

Early in 1996, Hillary's book *It Takes a Village* was published and became a best-seller. Its audiotape version won a Grammy Award. Hillary explained that she wrote the

Accepting her Grammy award for the audio version of It Takes a Village *(Landov)*

book to find out "how we can make our society into the kind of village that enables children to grow into able, caring, resilient adults."

The book offered sound advice on commonplace subjects, such as making sure the television set is not constantly on, making time to read aloud to children of any age, and seeing that spiritual development grows along with intellectual development. In the book, Hillary expressed opinions on more complex subjects as well. She proposed ideas she had advanced years earlier on the government's responsibility for the welfare of all children. She emphasized the importance of federal regulation of day-care centers and talked about the effects of failed marriages on children.

A tour to talk about the book and autograph copies took Hillary across the country visiting major bookstores and meeting thousands of admiring readers.

A Grand Jury and Two Bombshells

By January 1996, the independent prosecutor, Kenneth Starr, had gathered enough evidence on the subject of Whitewater to present to a grand jury in U.S. District Court in Washington. The grand jury would then study the evidence to decide whether to bring formal charges in the case. Hillary was summoned to testify on January 26 and spent about four hours answering questions.

Next came a double bombshell. Travelgate investigators obtained an unsent memo written by David Watkins at the time of the travel office firings in 1993. It said the first lady had ordered him to fire the travel office staff and there would have been "hell to pay" if he had "failed to take swift and decisive action in conformity with the First Lady's wishes." Republicans as well as columnists and commentators praised Watkins, but shortly, under oath in the Congressional Whitewater hearings, he denied that Hillary had ordered the firings.

Chelsea, Bill, and Hillary Clinton at the Democratic National Convention in Chicago, 1996 (Associated Press)

The second bombshell exploded as Hillary's executive assistant, Carolyn Huber, revealed that in August 1995 she had found a computer printout in a White House book room but had never looked at it. Now, stirred by the grand jury investigation, she looked. The printout was the Rose firm's billing records on Whitewater that the Senate investigators had sought for two years. Two pages, one of which detailed Hillary's time spent on Castle Grande (which Hillary had denied working for, under oath), contained Hillary's fingerprints.

Hillary's critics said that if she hid the records in the White House to hinder the Senate's Whitewater investigation, she had literally committed a crime. Others pointed out that before Vince Foster's suicide, Huber had often handled papers and files in his office and might have moved the printout to the White House book room without even knowing she did it and without Hillary knowing about it.

More and more during the year, the American public was given the impression—whether it was right or wrong—that Hillary Rodham Clinton was at the heart of the scandal called Whitewater and its dishonest financial contracts. "Well, we know Hillary Clinton is a pivotal player," said Republican Senator Rod Grams of Minnesota. "I mean, everything kind of runs through her office and out of her office."

In May 1996 Hillary learned that Jim and Susan McDougal had been convicted of mail fraud and conspiracy for their plundering of the Madison Guaranty Savings & Loan, including the Castle Grande business. She also learned that McDougal, hoping to get a short jail sentence, was cooperating with prosecutors. The Associated Press reported an interview with him in which he implied that Webb Hubbell had done the Castle Grande legal work for which Hillary billed Madison Guaranty.

In Chicago that summer, the Democrats met to nominate Bill Clinton for his second term as president. There Hillary made her first speech on prime-time TV. Once again she proposed that "it takes a village to raise a child," describing new government orders and programs she recommended for controlling businesses that deal with families. She also pledged to keep pushing for universal health care.

11

WORLD TOURS AND CONTROVERSY

Hillary Rodham Clinton had worked hard to help her husband earn re-election. She made speeches all across America: on college campuses, at benefits for the Democratic Party, and before feminist groups. One of her distinct achievements was that she raised a total of $11.3 million, mostly from women, to support the campaign. And now, while no other Democratic president since Franklin D. Roosevelt had been elected to a second term in office, Bill Clinton had won another four years in the White House.

Right after the election, the first family made a brief tour across the Pacific. In an official appearance in Australia's Sydney Opera House, Hillary spoke to an enthusiastic audience on "Women of the Twenty-first Century." At a reception after the speech, she insisted on finding members of Australia's Labor Party so she could discuss their views on health care and affirmative action.

Later, chatting with a *Time* magazine reporter, Hillary mentioned her plans to play a "formal role" in welfare reform during the new administration. But by the time the first family's tour reached Manila, White House press secretary Mike McCurry was telling inquisitive reporters, "I am not aware that there is any formal role that is planned for the first lady."

Managers in the first lady's White House office found that it now took two speechwriters to keep up with her, and tracking her favorite projects was almost a full-time job for one assistant. Pushing her "reading initiative," she read aloud to District of Columbia schoolchildren. In Philadelphia, she and Bill, with Vice President Al Gore and his wife, Tipper, helped launch General Colin Powell's Volunteerism Summit. Looking ahead to the year 2000, Hillary introduced the Millennium Project, a seemingly limitless activity that included everything from producing "Millennium Moment" TV spots to sending robots to Mars to preserving the original American flag in the Smithsonian.

For Christmas 1997, Hillary gave Bill a chocolate-colored Labrador dog named Buddy, who quickly became the archenemy of Socks, the family cat. Children wrote thousands of letters to, and about, the White House pets. Hillary published some in her book *Dear Socks, Dear Buddy* and gave the income to the National Park Foundation.

A Busy Year at Age 50

In 1997 Hillary traveled around the world. In March, she and Chelsea spent two weeks in Africa, meeting with women leaders in five different nations. In August, the first lady flew to London to represent the president and the United States at the funeral of England's Princess Diana, who had been killed in an automobile accident. There she met the American-born Queen Noor of Jordan, who had been active in supporting two of Diana's favorite causes, the International Campaign to Ban Landmines and the Landmine Survivors' Network. Hillary and Queen Noor became good friends.

At the summer's end, Hillary had to face an uncomfortable reality she had known for months: Chelsea was going off to college. Despite her mother's urging her to choose a school near Washington, the 18-year-old had applied to, and been accepted by, Stanford University in California. Both of Chelsea's parents knew how much they would miss her, but they encouraged her steps toward independence.

Argentina was Hillary's next destination. In a speech there in October, she saw a crowd of activist women rise in a standing ovation when she strongly recommended the use of birth control. Roman Catholics, however, who are many in Argentina, were offended.

October 26, 1997, marked Hillary's 50th birthday. During a week of celebration, cover photos on *Time* and *U.S. News & World Report* saluted her. *A&E Biography* did a TV special about her. At the White House, staffers set up a series of booths depicting each decade of her life and also threw a big party at a Washington hotel. In Chicago, high school bands met her at O'Hare Airport and Mayor Richard M. Daley named a park for her before she went to Park Ridge for Hillary Rodham Clinton Day. At Park Ridge, old friends gathered at her elementary school for a "This is your life" session remembering childhood and the early teachings of the Rev. Don Jones in his University of Life.

November saw Hillary in Belfast, Ireland, then meeting with British prime minister Tony Blair at his

country home at Chequers, England. They were joined by U.S. Secretary of Housing and Urban Development

Hillary celebrates her 50th birthday on Oprah Winfrey's television show, 1997 (Landov)

Andrew M. Cuomo, Deputy Secretary of the Treasury Lawrence Summers, and Democratic Leadership Council President Al From. With leaders of Blair's Labour Party, they discussed promotion of The Third Way, a political party or idea that uses government to control a mix of free enterprise and socialism.

Later in November, Hillary toured Central Asia and Russia, where she concentrated once again on a favorite subject by visiting hospitals and other facilities for newborns and infants.

Groups of children were invited to the White House East Room on January 7, 1998, to hear President Clinton announce "the largest single commitment to child care in the history of the United States." He was sending to Congress his proposed day-care bill. "I thank my wife," he said, "who has been talking to me about all these things for twenty-five years now, and is sitting here thinking that I have finally got around to doing what she has been telling me to do."

Monica Lewinsky

Early in the morning on Wednesday, January 21, 1998, Hillary was awakened by her husband. "You're not going to believe this," he said, "but—I want to tell you what's in the newspapers."

The newspapers—and the TV and radio reporters—were telling the world about a six-hour deposition that

Bill Clinton had made the preceding Saturday to lawyers for Paula Corbin Jones. (A deposition is testimony given to lawyers by a person under oath to tell the truth.) Jones was the former Arkansas state employee who, three years earlier, had sued Bill Clinton for sexual harassment.

Hillary learned that Jones's lawyers, in taking down the deposition, had asked President Clinton about numbers of girlfriends with whom, they believed, he had been intimate over many years. The lawyers referred to them as "Jane Does"—a name used by lawyers when they either don't know or don't want to reveal a person's real name. It was revealed that Jane Doe Number Six was a young woman named Monica Lewinsky, who had served as an intern on the president's White House staff and had later been transferred to duties at the Pentagon. The Jones lawyers listed her as a potential witness in their case.

Later that morning, Hillary learned that during the deposition Bill had denied having intimate relations with Lewinsky and had been questioned about gifts he had given to her. One was a copy of *Leaves of Grass* by Walt Whitman. "He gave me that same book," the first lady told an assistant, "after our second date."

A Vast Right-wing Conspiracy

On the following Tuesday, Hillary appeared on NBC television's *Today* show. Host Matt Lauer asked about the president's gifts to Lewinsky. "Anyone who knows my husband," replied Hillary, "knows that he is an extremely generous person to people he knows, to strangers, to anybody who is around him. And I think that, you know, his behavior, his treatment of people, will certainly explain all of this. I mean, I've seen him take his tie off and hand it to somebody."

As Lauer asked why many people seemed to dislike the president, the first lady said, "I don't know what it is about my husband that generates such hostility. But I have seen it for twenty-five years." She then said his problems could be blamed on "this vast right-wing conspiracy that has been conspiring against my husband since the day he announced for president."

With the world clamoring for more sensational news from the White House, Hillary went about her business as first lady. In Davos, Switzerland, in February, she spoke before the World Economic Forum. Next she visited Jordan to renew her friendship with Queen Noor. In May she returned to Switzerland to accept a $40,000 prize from the World Health Organization for her work for children and women. She gave the money (which had been donated by the United Arab Emirates) to a charity that strove to reduce infant mortality.

By the summer of 1998, there seemed to be no one in the world who did not know the name Monica Lewinsky, and very few did not know the name Kenneth Starr. As the independent prosecutor, he had turned the attention of the Whitewater investigators from questionable bank and real estate deals in Arkansas to the president's personal behavior in the White House.

Starr's committee summoned the president before a federal grand jury on August 17, 1998. There Bill Clinton gave testimony about the truth of his deposition to the Paula Jones lawyers. That evening, he appeared on nationwide television. "I did have a relationship with Miss Lewinsky that was not appropriate," he said. "In fact, it was wrong. It constituted a critical lapse in judgment and a personal failure on my part, for which I am solely and completely responsible."

The first lady's friends sensed that she was angry. They knew how frustrated she had been by the ultimate collapse of her plan for reforming health care. They had watched her work to build her standing worldwide as a defender of women's and children's rights. They understood that she hoped and planned for a major career after the White House years. They realized that the devastating headlines and on-the-air bulletins were not only personally painful to Hillary but could set her back politically.

At the White House, the first lady's spokesperson, Marsha Berry, told reporters that Mrs. Clinton's husband had "misled" her along with the rest of the nation, but that Hillary herself had not misled the public.

Persistent as always, Hillary kept to her official schedule. Late in August she was in Belfast, Ireland, for a conference on "Vital Voices: Women in Democracy," which encouraged women to participate in public life. A similar conference came in September in Montevideo, Uruguay, during Hillary's 10-day tour of Latin America. With the fall elections, she campaigned in New York to help Democrat Charles Schumer win Alfonse D'Amato's Senate seat and in California to help Barbara Boxer retain hers.

Articles of Impeachment

On September 9, Starr and the Whitewater investigating committee released a 453-page report to the House of Representatives. It described details of Bill Clinton's relationship with Monica Lewinsky and accused him of "abundant and calculating" lies. The report did not mention Whitewater, the subject that the independent prosecutor and his committee had been authorized to investigate. The president's attorneys responded with a 78-page rebuttal.

Hillary stood by her husband. On November 13, Bill Clinton's lawyers made an agreement with Paula Corbin Jones's lawyers: The president would not apologize for or admit to sexual harassment, but agreed to pay $850,000 cash to settle the matter.

Now Hillary was aware that the Judiciary Committee of the U.S. House of Representatives, after reviewing the Starr report, was debating whether to recommend, to the full House, the impeachment of her husband.

The United States Constitution's Article II says: "The President, Vice President and all civil Officers of the United States, shall be removed from Office on Impeachment for, and Conviction of, Treason, Bribery, or other high Crimes and Misdemeanors." Under laws made later, any decision to impeach a president has to be made by the House of Representatives.

On December 12, after seven days of extensive arguments over whether or not Bill Clinton had committed high crimes and misdemeanors, the Judiciary Committee decided that he had. And on Saturday, December 19, the House voted, almost entirely along party lines, to approve two articles of impeachment. (An "article" in this usage is a brief statement that defines a specific matter or issue.) The first article stated that the president had tried to obstruct justice by making false statements. The second article claimed he had committed perjury—that is, he had lied under oath—in his testimonies to the Starr grand jury and to the Jones lawyers. For only the second time in United States history, and for the first time in 130 years, the country's president was impeached.

That Saturday afternoon, Democratic members of Congress hurried to the White House lawn for a rally showing their support of Bill Clinton, who greeted them there. Standing at his side was Hillary Rodham Clinton.

12

FROM IMPEACHMENT TO THE SENATE

At the trial of impeachment of a U.S. president, the Senate serves as the jury, with the chief justice of the Supreme Court of the United States presiding as judge, and with members of the House serving as prosecutors. Conviction requires a two-thirds majority of the Senate's 100 members.

The Impeachment Trial

Starting on Thursday, January 7, 1999, a worldwide television audience watched the Clinton impeachment trial for five weeks. Prosecutors tried to prove that Bill Clinton had lied to investigators rather than admit to his relationship with Monica Lewinsky.

Hillary waited quietly through the five weeks. On January 20, 1999, in the middle of the trial, she was sitting in the gallery at a joint session of Congress as the president delivered his annual State of the Union message. His speech included a comment on Hillary's crusade to preserve the original "Star-Spangled Banner." Then he said, "I'd like to take just a minute to honor her, for leading our millennium project, for all she has done for our children. I honor her. Thank you. And here she is." A burst of applause saluted the first lady.

The nightmare ended on Friday, February 12, when 45 senators voted guilty and 55 not guilty on the perjury charge. The vote was 50 to 50 on obstruction of justice. Neither vote came close to the majority of 66 needed for conviction.

Looking to the Future

Hillary had turned 51 in October 1998. She knew that she and Bill would be leaving the White House at the end of his term on January 20, 2001. During the impeachment trial and the weeks leading up to it, she thought about where they might go and what they might do in the years ahead. Now, with the trial over, she could give serious attention to future possibilities.

Two facts kept bouncing around in her mind. One was something New York congressman Charlie Rangel—an old

Throughout her husband's impeachment proceedings, Hillary stood by and showed unwavering support. (Landov)

friend she had known since they both served on the Watergate committee—had said just after the fall elections. Politicians from Illinois, he told her, were talking about getting her to run for the Senate. "Why not New York?" he asked.

The second fact was that New York's senior senator, Democrat Daniel Patrick Moynihan, had announced that he would not seek re-election in 2000. This would create a good opportunity for Hillary to pursue the vacant office.

Looking ahead, Hillary concentrated on another makeover. Working out painstakingly on White House gym equipment, she saw her weight come down. A short, feminine hairdo and advice from clothing designer Oscar de la Renta gave her up-to-the-minute style.

Talk about Hillary as a candidate for a seat in the U.S. Senate began in January 1999 on such Sunday morning

TV programs as *Meet the Press*. Democrat Charles Schumer had just captured the seat held by Republican Al D'Amato. Democratic Party leaders were eager to find a strong contender to succeed Moynihan. They liked that in the elections of the fall of 1998 the first lady had worked hard for Democratic candidates, touring 20 states to speak at 34 rallies and 50 fund-raisers. She had also recorded some 100 telemarketing messages. More than half of those she helped were winners. Public opinion polls showed that 70 percent of people surveyed said they approved of her.

Key Democrats in New York State began talking to Hillary about running. One of them was Harold Ickes. He had been Bill Clinton's deputy chief of staff in the White House, and his father had been Secretary of the Interior under President Franklin D. Roosevelt. Through the spring of 1999, Ickes, himself a wise and perceptive politician, often talked with the first lady about the pros and cons of a Senate race. In late May, she phoned him. "I'm doing this," she said.

Ickes later explained why he thought she decided to run. "She didn't want to work for anyone," he said. "She wasn't interested in money. She didn't care for the lecture circuit. She had no passion for academe or foundations. She said to me that being one out of one hundred, she could have a tremendous impact on shaping policy."

Official Announcement

Senator Moynihan owned a 900-acre farm in the crossroads town of Pindars Corners, near Oneonta in upstate New York. He invited Hillary there to announce on July 7 that she was running. A crowd of reporters estimated at 250 trampled the rural grounds, and two dozen satellite trucks beamed picture and sound worldwide as Hillary said, "I suppose the questions on everyone's mind are: Why the Senate? Why New York? And why me?" Agreeing that these were fair questions, she went on: "I think I have some real work to do to get out and listen and learn from the people of New York and demonstrate that what I'm for is maybe as important, if not more important, than where I'm from."

Hillary began her campaign for the Senate with what she called a "listening tour" of the state. It took her not only to the big cities but to small towns in every county. It helped her to understand the everyday problems, frustrations, and joys of the folks who lived on the side streets and back roads and worked in the stores and on the farms. And it gave her some learning experiences. In the mostly Republican village of Albion, New York, for example, she and her entourage had lunch in a local coffee shop. Headlines and a *New York Times* photograph next day told the world that, while the coffee-shop owner had provided the meal "on the house," Hillary had left no tip for the waitress. She did not make that mistake again.

By August, it seemed clear that Hillary's Republican opponent would be New York mayor Rudolph Giuliani, who was endorsed by Governor George Pataki. A Brooklyn native who had earned the mayoralty by his work as a tough, no-holds-barred prosecutor, Giuliani was admired for his success as mayor in reducing crime in the nation's biggest city.

A New York State Home

Any member of the U.S. Senate or House of Representatives must have a residence in the state he or she represents. Thus, busy as she was on her listening tour and keeping up with her duties as first lady, Hillary had to go house-hunting. In Chappaqua, a New York City suburb in Westchester County, she and Bill found a comfortable older home on a dead-end street. It even had a barn that was renovated to become headquarters for the Secret Service agents who were always on duty. In January 2000, the Clintons moved in.

Late-night television host David Letterman pleaded with Hillary's staff for a month or more trying to get her to appear on his show. On January 12, 2000, she was there. As a Chappaqua neighbor, he steered the conversation to the Clintons' new home, then said, "Every idiot in the area is going to drive by honking now."

"Oh," said Hillary, "was that you?"

The audience, along with Letterman, howled with laughter. The appearance, Hillary realized, brought her more notice and support than a dozen speeches might have.

Building Another Campaign

By mid-May, opinion polls showed Hillary ahead of Giuliani in voters' thinking. On May 16, the New York State Democratic convention in Albany formally nominated her as candidate for the U.S. Senate. Only three days later, on May 19, Mayor Giuliani announced that he had been diagnosed with prostate cancer and was withdrawing from the race.

The Republicans nominated Rick Lazio, who had represented Long Island's Suffolk County in the U.S. House of Representatives since 1993, to run against Hillary. He immediately launched a hard-hitting campaign, appearing 16 times in four upstate cities on his first full day as a candidate.

On August 14 in Los Angeles, Hillary spoke before the opening session of the Democratic National Convention that had gathered to nominate Vice President Al Gore for president and Senator Joe Lieberman for vice president. "Bill and I are closing one chapter of our lives," she said, "and soon, we'll be starting a new one. Thank you for giving me the most extraordinary opportunity to work here at home and around the world on the issues that matter most to children, women, and families, for your support and faith in good times—and in bad. Thank you for the honor and blessing of a lifetime."

Hillary had to face debates with her opponent Lazio. In the first, in Buffalo on September 13, NBC's Tim Russert brought up the Monica Lewinsky story and showed the videotape from Hillary's appearance on the *Today* show. He asked if she regretted "misleading the American people" and if she would apologize for "branding people as part of a vast right-wing conspiracy."

"I've tried to be as forthcoming as I could, given the circumstances," Hillary replied. "Obviously I didn't mislead anyone. I didn't know the truth. My husband has certainly acknowledged that he did mislead the country as well as his family."

An End to Whitewater

Independent prosecutor Kenneth Starr's Whitewater investigation, which had cost U.S. taxpayers $40 million, officially ended the preceding June 30th when the law that created it expired. On September 20, 2000, independent counsel Robert W. Ray of Starr's staff filed a final report to the U.S. District Court of Appeals. It said there was not enough evidence to show that either Bill or Hillary Clinton had been involved in any criminal behavior in the Whitewater deals and that no proof was found that they had obstructed justice or concealed information from investigators.

Victory

Journalists began to notice a change in Hillary's attitude. They saw her eagerly greeting crowds for as long as three hours a day, shaking every hand that reached from restraining ropes, stopping with a smile for snapshot-takers—all a big worry to the Secret Service people, who had never seen her mix into a throng. But it was only through meeting and interacting with so many New Yorkers that Hillary learned what was on the voters' minds and how she could help them if she was elected to the Senate.

A second debate with Lazio came on Sunday, October 8, at WCBS-TV in New York. Closing it, Hillary read from a fund-raising letter her opponent had mailed. It asked people to contribute to his campaign because of only "six words: I'm running against Hillary Rodham Clinton."

"New Yorkers deserve more than that," said Hillary. "How about seven words? How about jobs, education, health, Social Security, environment, choice?" On Sunday, October 22, the influential *New York Times* endorsed Hillary as its choice for Senator.

The campaign was tough and at times quite turbulent, but Hillary continued to win support throughout the state. On November 7, 2000, 55 percent of New York State's voters elected Hillary Rodham Clinton to a six-year term as United States Senator.

13

THE JUNIOR SENATOR FROM NEW YORK

The day after her victory, a relaxed and smiling Hillary held a press conference. Among the many questions about how she managed to win by more than 800,000 votes, one reporter wanted to know if she was thinking about the presidency of the United States. "No," she replied, "I'm going to serve my six years as the junior senator from New York." (The senator most recently elected in each state is called the junior senator.)

In mid-December, two weeks before she was sworn in as a senator, Hillary announced that she had signed a contract with publisher Simon & Schuster to write her memoirs, for which she would be paid $8 million. The book contract meant that for at least the next couple of years Hillary would have two jobs: senator and writer.

Hillary's last few weeks in the White House were not without controversy. Her husband took advantage of a departing president's freedom to grant pardons as he sees fit. Critics noted that many of those pardoned were clients of the first lady's lawyer-brother Hugh Rodham, who was living in the White House at this time. Hillary said she knew nothing about the pardons.

Soon Hillary and Bill bought a house in Washington. That gave her not only a place to go home to at night but a setting for the entertaining that a former first lady who is a U.S. senator would be expected to do.

The Senator Goes to Work

New York's Senator Clinton introduced her first legislative bill on February 19, 2001, when she proposed a federal package to boost the economy of upstate New York. Her bill was the first of seven that kept her campaign promise to make strengthening the upstate economy her first priority.

By midsummer 2001, a columnist for a major newspaper reported that Hillary "has gained mostly good marks for hard work and success at becoming ordinary. Her days are full of talk of salt mines, sewers, and brownfields. Gone are the protesters and the hordes of reporters. She still has her Secret Service detail, but they're far more relaxed, and sometimes even smile. She's quick with a joke, and even gives the occasional slap on the back."

Then came September 11, 2001. Within 24 hours, Senator Clinton was looking at lower Manhattan's smoking rubble. "I was totally unprepared for what I saw," she said. "The damage, the mountain of burning wreckage, the smell, just was overwhelming." She set about helping to organize federal aid for the city and the victims—especially some 10,000 children who lost one or both parents and, she said, were "victims of war." She urged Congress to back stronger anti-terrorism laws and federal control of airport baggage-screening.

In August 2002, when war on Iraq seemed likely, Hillary urged President Bush to seek Congressional approval before any attack. "I want to be sure we debate it," she said, "and then as a nation we'll stand behind the decision."

In the fall, antiwar protesters handed out leaflets outside Hillary's New York office, staged an eight-hour sit-in there, picketed a speech she made, and flooded her phone lines with calls. On October 11, she voted with most of Congress to authorize the president to take military action against Iraq.

Just before Christmas 2002, former presidential candidate Al Gore said he would not run again in 2004. A CNN/*Time* magazine poll asked registered Democrats whom they would nominate. Hillary won 30 percent of those surveyed, while former vice-presidential candidate Joe Lieberman of Connecticut and Senator John Kerry of Massachusetts each got 13 percent.

Despite all the presidential rumors, Hillary continued her work in Washington, where she was earning a reputation as a busy, active senator, especially given her lack of seniority. Before 2003 she was serving on the Senate's Environment and Public Works Committee and its Health, Education, Labor and Pensions Committee. In 2003 she became the first New York senator to serve on a key panel: the Senate Armed Services Committee.

Living History

Eager book-buyers lined up overnight in New York City on June 8, 2003, to be the first to get Hillary's memoirs the next morning. One million copies had been printed. The author appeared at bookstores and autographed copies until her fingers ached and then signed more books day after day at store after store.

Hillary said that the book was titled *Living History* "because I was very privileged to live history in the White House for eight years. It's about those White House years." Reporters noted that, while Hillary had spent two years writing the book, she had been helped by author Maryanne Vollers, by her White House speech writer Lissa Muscatine, and by researcher Ruby Shamir. Hillary acknowledged all three, and many other helpers, in the last of the book's 562 pages.

On CNN's political talk show *Crossfire*, commentator Tucker Carlson belittled the chances of Hillary's book selling 1 million copies. "If they sell a million copies," he said, "I'll eat my shoes."

By July 9, one month after publication, 1 million copies had been sold. That afternoon, apparently without warning to Carlson, Senator Clinton walked into the studio while the program was being broadcast. Before a cheering audience, she presented Carlson with a chocolate cake in the shape of a brown boot. As Carlson picked up a knife and fork, someone asked which part of the shoe he would start with. "Well, obviously," he said, "the heel."

Hillary celebrates the much-anticipated release of her memoirs, Living History, *in 2003.* (Associated Press)

TIME LINE

1947 Born on October 26 in Chicago

1961 Participates in "University of Life" sponsored by the Rev. Don Jones

1962 Hears the Rev. Martin Luther King Jr. preach

1964 In high school, heads Students for Barry Goldwater (Republican candidate for U.S. presidency)

1965 Enters Wellesley College in Massachusetts; as a freshman, is elected president of the Young Republicans Club

1967 Becomes a Democrat

1968 Attends the Democratic National Convention in Chicago; is elected president of college government; interviews the radical thinker Saul Alinsky and writes her senior thesis on his ideas

1969 Earns a standing ovation for her speech at the Wellesley graduation and is pictured in *LIFE* magazine; enters Yale Law School

1970 Negotiates between Yale administrators and protesters over the Bobby Seale-Black Panthers trial; works with mentor Marian Wright Edelman; holds a summer internship in the Children's Defense Fund in Washington; studies in the Yale Child Study Center; meets Bill Clinton

1972 Speaks at a meeting of the Democratic National Committee's platform committee

1973 Graduates from Yale Law School; takes the Arkansas bar exam

1974 Serves on the legal staff planning the impeachment of President Richard M. Nixon; moves to Arkansas to teach at the University of Arkansas Law School

1975 Marries Bill Clinton on October 11 and keeps the name Hillary Rodham

1976 Joins the Rose Law Firm; Bill Clinton is elected attorney general of Arkansas

1977 Appointed to the Legal Services Corporation by President Jimmy Carter

1978   Co-signs a mortgage note for the Whitewater Development Company; begins trading in commodities futures; Bill Clinton is elected governor of Arkansas

1979   Moves into the governor's mansion as first lady of Arkansas; organizes the Governor's School; ends commodities trading with a profit

1980   Daughter Chelsea is born February 27; Bill loses his campaign for re-election

1982   Decides to be known as Hillary Rodham Clinton or Mrs. Clinton; Bill wins the governorship again

1983   Heads a commission to recommend improvements in the Arkansas school system

1984   Bill is re-elected governor

1985   Accepts Jim McDougal, head of the Whitewater Development Company, as a client

1986   Bill wins again as the governor's term changes from two to four years

1987   Chairs the American Bar Association committee on equal participation of women and minorities in the legal profession

1990 Bill is re-elected governor; Hillary starts organizing support for his nomination in 1992 for president

1991 Appears on *60 Minutes* following tabloid newspaper reports on Bill's extramarital affairs

1992 Bill Clinton is elected president of the United States

1993 Moves into the White House as first lady; is instrumental in decisions on appointments to the president's cabinet and staff; is appointed chairman of the president's National Task Force on Health Care; is blamed for Travelgate firings; Vince Foster commits suicide; the Clintons face Whitewater investigation

1994 Paula Corbin Jones sues President Clinton for sexual harassment; Hillary's health care plan dies in Congress

1995 Testifies before the Resolution Trust Company investigating the Madison Guaranty Savings & Loan bank; speaks in China at the United Nations' Fourth International Conference on Women

1996 Publishes her book *It Takes A Village*; testifies on Whitewater before a federal grand jury; missing Rose Law Firm billing records are found in the White House living quarters; speaks at the Democratic National Convention nominating Bill for a second term; after his re-election, speaks in Australia

1997 Heads the Clinton administration's "Millennium Project" for the year 2000; publishes her book *Dear Socks, Dear Buddy*; as first lady, tours Africa, England, Argentina, Ireland, Central Asia, Russia

1998 Monica Lewinsky named a potential witness in sexual harassment lawsuit against Bill Clinton; on the NBC *Today* show, Hillary cites a "vast right-wing conspiracy" against her husband; visits Switzerland and Jordan

1999 Bill Clinton impeached and found not guilty; Hillary runs for New York senator

2000 Buys home in Chappaqua, New York; Whitewater committee finds no criminal activity or obstruction of justice; elected senator on November 7; signs a contract to write her memoirs

2001 Introduces her first Senate bill; visits the World Trade Center disaster site

2002 Votes to authorize President Bush to use military action against Iraq

2003 Publishes her memoir *Living History*, selling 1 million copies in the first month

HOW TO BECOME A LAWYER

THE JOB

Lawyers give legal advice and represent clients in court when necessary. No matter what their specialty, their job is to help clients know their rights under the law and then help them achieve those rights before a judge, jury, government agency, or other legal forum, such as an arbitration panel. Lawyers may represent businesses and individuals. For businesses, they manage tax matters, arrange for stock to be issued, handle claims cases, represent the firm in real estate dealings, and advise on all legal matters. For individuals they may be trustees, guardians, or executors; they may draw up wills or contracts or advise on income taxes or on the purchase or sale of a home. Some lawyers work solely in the courts; others carry on most of their business outside of court, doing such tasks as drawing up mortgages, deeds, contracts, and other legal documents or handling the background work necessary for court cases, which might include researching cases in a law library or interviewing witnesses. A number of lawyers work to establish and enforce laws for the federal and state governments by drafting legislation, representing the government in court, or serving as judges.

Lawyers can also take positions as professors in law schools. Administrators, research workers, and writers are also important to the profession. Administrative positions in business or government may be of a nonlegal nature, but the qualities, background, and experience of a lawyer are often helpful in such positions.

Other individuals with legal training may choose not to practice but instead opt for careers in which their background and knowledge of law are important. These careers include tax collectors, credit investigators, FBI agents, insurance adjusters, process servers, and probation officers.

Some of the specialized fields for lawyers include the following:

Civil lawyers work in a field also known as private law. They focus on damage suits and breach-of-contract suits; prepare and draw up deeds, leases, wills, mortgages, and contracts; and act as trustees, guardians, or executors of an estate when necessary.

Criminal lawyers, also known as *defense lawyers,* specialize in cases dealing with offenses committed against society or the state, such as theft, murder, or arson. They interview clients and witnesses to ascertain facts in a case, correlate their findings with known cases, and prepare a case to defend a client against the charges made. They conduct a defense at the trial, examine witnesses, and summarize the case with a closing argument to a jury.

District attorneys, also known as *prosecuting attorneys,* represent the city, county, state, or federal government in court proceedings. They gather and analyze evidence and review legal material relevant to a lawsuit. Then they present their case to the grand jury, which decides whether the evidence is sufficient for an indictment. If it is not, the suit is dismissed and there is no trial. If the grand jury decides to indict the accused, however, the case goes to court, where the district attorney appears before the judge and jury to present evidence against the defendant.

Probate lawyers specialize in planning and settling estates. They draw up wills, deeds of trust, and similar documents for clients who want to plan the distribution of their belongings among their heirs when they die. Upon a client's death, probate lawyers vouch for the validity of the will and represent the executors and administrators of the estate.

Bankruptcy attorneys assist their clients, both individuals and corporations, in obtaining protection from creditors under existing bankruptcy laws and with financial reorganization and debt repayment.

Corporation lawyers advise corporations concerning their legal rights, obligations, or privileges. They study constitutions, statutes, previous decisions, ordinances, and decisions of quasi-judicial bodies that are applicable to corporations. They advise corporations on the pros and cons of prosecuting or defending a lawsuit. They act as agent of the corporation in various transactions and seek to keep clients from expensive litigation.

Maritime lawyers, sometimes referred to as *admiralty lawyers,* specialize in laws regulating commerce and navigation on the high seas and any navigable waters, including inland lakes and rivers. Although there is a general maritime law, it operates in each country according to that country's courts, laws, and customs. Maritime law covers contracts, insurance, property damage, and personal injuries.

Intellectual property lawyers focus on helping their clients with patents, trademarks, and copyright protection. *Patent lawyers* are intellectual property lawyers who specialize in securing patents for inventors from the United States Patent Office and prosecuting or defending suits of patent infringements. They prepare detailed specifications for the patent and may organize a corporation or advise an existing corporation to commercialize on a patent. Biotechnology patent law is a further specialization of patent law. *Biotechnology patent lawyers* specialize in helping biotechnology researchers, scientists, and research corporations with all legal aspects of their biotechnology patents.

Elder law attorneys specialize in providing legal services for the elderly and, in some cases, the disabled.

Tax attorneys handle cases resulting from problems of inheritance, income tax, estate tax, franchises, and real estate tax, among other things.

Insurance attorneys advise insurance companies about legal matters pertaining to insurance transactions. They approve the wording of insurance policies, review the legality of claims against the company, and draw up legal documents.

An *international lawyer* specializes in the body of rules observed by nations in their relations with one another. Some of these laws have been agreed to in treaties; others have evolved from long-standing customs and traditions.

Securities and exchange lawyers monitor the activities of individuals and corporations involved in trading and oversee to make sure they comply with applicable laws. When corporations undergo takeovers and mergers, securities and exchange lawyers are there to represent the corporations' interests and fulfill all legal obligations involved in the transaction.

Real estate lawyers handle the transfer of property and perform such duties as searching public records and deeds to establish titles of property, holding funds for investment in escrow accounts, and acting as trustees of property. They draw up legal documents and act as agents in various real estate transactions.

Title attorneys deal with titles, leases, contracts, and other legal documents pertaining to the ownership of land, as well as gas, oil, and mineral rights. They prepare documents to cover the purchase or sale of such property and rights, examine documents to determine ownership, advise organizations about legal requirements concerning titles, and participate in the trial or lawsuits in connection with titles.

It is important to note that once you are licensed to practice law, you are legally qualified to practice any one or more of these and many other specialties. Some *general practitioners* handle both criminal and civil matters of all sorts. To become licensed, you must be admitted to the bar of that state. *Bar examiners* test the qualifications of applicants. They prepare and administer written exams covering legal subjects, examine candidates orally, and recommend admission of those who meet the prescribed standards.

REQUIREMENTS
High School
A high school diploma, a college degree, and three years of law school are minimum requirements for a law degree. A high school diploma is a first step on the ladder of education that a lawyer must climb. If you are considering a career in

law, courses such as government, history, social studies, and economics provide a solid background for entering college-level courses. Speech courses are also helpful for building strong communication skills necessary for the profession. Also take advantage of any computer-related classes or experience you can get, because lawyers and judges often use technology to research and interpret the law, from surfing the Internet to searching legal databases.

Postsecondary Training

To enter any law school approved by the American Bar Association, you must satisfactorily complete at least three, and usually four, years of college work. Most law schools do not specify any particular courses for prelaw education. Usually a liberal arts track, with courses in English, history, economics, social sciences, logic, and public speaking, is most advisable. A college student planning on specialization in a particular area of law, however, might also take courses significantly related to that area, such as economics, agriculture, or political science. Students interested in a law career should write to several law schools to learn more about any requirements and to see if the schools will accept credits from the college the student is planning to attend.

Currently, more than 185 law schools in the United States are approved by the American Bar Association; others, many of them night schools, are approved by state authorities only. Most of the approved law schools, however, do have night sessions to accommodate part-time students. Part-time courses of study usually take four years.

Law school training consists of required courses such as legal writing and research, contracts, criminal law, constitutional law, torts, and property. The second and third years of law school may be devoted to specialized courses of interest to the student, such as evidence, business transactions and corporations, or admiralty. The study of cases and decisions is of central importance to the law student, who will be required to read and study thousands of these cases. A degree of juris doctor (J.D.) or bachelor of laws (LL.B.) is usually granted upon graduation. Some law students considering specialization, research, or teaching may go on for advanced study.

Most law schools require that applicants take the Law School Admission Test (LSAT), where prospective law students are tested on their critical thinking, writing, and reasoning abilities.

Certification or Licensing

Every state requires that lawyers be admitted to the bar of that state before they can practice. They require that applicants graduate from an approved law school and that they pass a written examination in the state in which they intend to practice. In a few states, graduates of law schools within the state are excused from these written examinations. After lawyers have been admitted to the bar in one state, they can practice in another state without taking a written examination if the states have reciprocity agreements; however, they will be required to meet certain state standards of good character and legal experience and pay any applicable fees.

Other Requirements

Federal courts and agencies have their own rules regulating admission to practice. Other requirements vary among the states. For example, Vermont, New York, Washington, Virginia, California, Maine, and Wyoming allow a person who has spent several years reading law in a law office but has no college training or who has a combination of reading and law school experience to take the state bar examination. Few people now enter law practice in this manner.

A few states accept the study of law by correspondence. Some states require that newly graduated lawyers serve a period of clerkship in an established law firm before they are eligible to take the bar examination.

All lawyers have to be effective communicators, work well with people, and be able to find creative solutions to problems, such as complex court cases.

EXPLORING

There are several ways in which you can learn more about a legal career. First, sit in on a trial or two at your local or state courthouse. Try to focus mainly on the judge and the lawyer and take note of what they do. Write down questions you have and terms or actions you don't understand. Then talk to your guidance counselor and ask for help in setting up a telephone or in-person interview with a judge or lawyer. Prepare a list of questions before your conversation to help focus your thoughts. Also, talk to your guidance counselor or political science teacher about starting or joining a shadowing program. Shadowing programs allow you to follow a person in a certain career around for a day or two to get an idea of what goes on in his or her typical day. You may even be invited to help out with a few minor duties.

You can also search the Internet for information about current court cases. Read court transcripts and summary opinions written by judges on issues of importance today. If you are still interested in law school after you've done some research, try to get a part-time job in a law office. Ask your guidance counselor for help.

If you are already in law school, you might consider becoming a student member of the American Library Association. Student members receive *Student Lawyer,* a magazine that contains useful information for aspiring lawyers. You can read sample articles from the magazine at http://www.abanet.org/lsd/stulawyer.

EMPLOYERS

About 75 percent of practicing lawyers in the United States work in private practice, either in law firms or alone. The others are employed in government, often at the local level. Lawyers working for the federal government hold positions in the Departments of Justice, Treasury, and Defense. Lawyers also hold positions as house counsel for public utilities, transportation companies, banks, insurance companies, real estate agencies, manufacturing firms, welfare and religious organizations, and other businesses and nonprofit organizations.

STARTING OUT

The first steps in entering the law profession are graduation from an approved law school and passing a state bar examination. Usually, beginning lawyers do not go into solo practice right away. It is often difficult to become established, and additional experience is helpful to the beginning lawyer. Also, most lawyers do not specialize in a particular branch of law without first gaining experience. Beginning lawyers usually work as assistants to experienced lawyers. At first they do mainly research and routine work. After a few years of successful experience, they may be ready to go out on their own. Other choices open to the beginning lawyer include joining an established law firm or entering a partnership with another lawyer. Positions are also available with banks, business corporations, insurance companies, private utilities, and a number of government agencies at different levels.

Many new lawyers are recruited directly from law school. Recruiters from law firms and other organizations come to the school and interview possible hires. Other new graduates can get job leads from local and state bar associations.

ADVANCEMENT

Lawyers with outstanding ability can expect to go a long way in their profession. Novice lawyers generally start as law clerks, but as they prove themselves and develop their abilities, many opportunities for advancement will arise. They may be promoted to junior partner in a law firm or establish their own practice. Lawyers may enter politics and become judges, mayors, congressmen, or other government leaders. Top positions are also available in business for the qualified lawyer. Lawyers working for the federal government advance according to the civil service system.

EARNINGS

Incomes generally increase as the lawyer gains experience and becomes better known in the field. The beginning lawyer in solo practice may barely make ends meet for the first few years. According to the National

Association for Law Placement, 2002 median salaries for new lawyers ranged from $53,500 for lawyers employed by firms of two to 25 attorneys to $118,000 for lawyers employed by firms of 501 or more attorneys. Those working for the government made approximately $40,000. Starting salaries for lawyers in business were $60,000. Recent graduates entering private practice made the most, earning approximately $80,000.

Experienced lawyers earn salaries that vary depending on the type, size, and location of their employers. According to the U.S. Department of Labor, the 2001 median salary for practicing lawyers was $88,760, although some senior partners earned well over $1 million a year. Ten percent earned less than $43,000. General attorneys in the federal government received $87,080 in 2000. State and local government attorneys generally made less, earning $64,190 and $66,280, respectively, in 2000.

WORK ENVIRONMENT

Offices and courtrooms are usually pleasant, although busy, places to work. Lawyers spend significant time in law libraries or record rooms, in the homes and offices of clients, and in prisons with clients or prospective witnesses. Unless they are directly involved in litigation, many lawyers never work in a courtroom.

Some courts, such as small claims, family, or surrogate, may have evening hours to provide flexibility to the community. Criminal arraignments may be held at any time of day or night. Court hours for most lawyers and judges are usually regular business hours, with a one-hour lunch break. Often, lawyers have to work long hours, spending evenings and weekends preparing cases and materials and working with clients. In addition to extensive work, the lawyer must always keep up with the latest developments in the profession. Also, it takes a long time to become a qualified lawyer, and it may be difficult to earn an adequate living until the lawyer gets enough experience to develop an established private practice.

Lawyers who are employed at law firms must often work grueling hours to advance in the firm. Spending long weekend hours doing research and interviewing people should be expected.

OUTLOOK

According to the *Occupational Outlook Handbook*, employment for lawyers is expected to grow at an average through rate the next decade, but record numbers of law school graduates have created strong competition for jobs, even though the number of graduates has begun to level off. Continued population growth, typical business activities, and increased numbers of legal cases involving health care, environmental, intellectual property, international law, elder law, and sexual harassment issues, among others, will create a steady demand for lawyers. Law services will be more accessible to the middle-income public with the popularity of prepaid legal services and clinics. However, stiff competition will continue to prompt lawyers to look for jobs in administrative, managerial, and business positions, where legal training is useful.

The top 10 percent of the graduating seniors of the country's best law schools will have more opportunities with well-known law firms and on legal staffs of corporations, in government agencies, and in law schools in the next few decades. Lawyers in solo practice will find it hard to earn a living until their practice is fully established. The best opportunities exist in small towns or suburbs of large cities, where there is less competition and new lawyers can meet potential clients more easily. Graduates with lower class standings and from lesser-known schools may have difficulty obtaining the most desirable positions. Banks, insurance companies, real estate firms, government agencies, and other organizations often hire law graduates. Legal positions in the armed forces are also available.

TO LEARN MORE ABOUT LAWYERS

BOOKS

Abrams, Lisa L. *The Official Guide to Legal Specialties.* Orlando, Fla.: Harcourt, 2000.

Echaore-McDavid, Susan. *Career Opportunities in Law and the Legal Industry.* New York: Facts On File, 2002.

Miller, Robert H. *Law School Confidential.* Irvine, Calif.: Griffin, 2000.

Noyes, Shanna Connell, and Henry S. Noyes. *Acing Your First Year of Law School.* Buffalo, N.Y.: William S. Hein & Co., 1999.

ORGANIZATIONS

For information about law student services offered by the ABA, contact

American Bar Association (ABA)

Service Center

541 North Fairbanks Court

Chicago, IL 60611

Tel: 312-988-5522

Email: abasvcctr@abanet.org

http://www.abanet.org

For information on workshops and seminars, contact

Association of American Law Schools

1201 Connecticut Avenue, NW, Suite 800

Washington, DC 20036-2605

Tel: 202-296-8851

Email: aals@aals.org

http://www.aals.org

The FBA provides information for lawyers and judges involved in federal practice.

Federal Bar Association (FBA)

Student Services

2215 M Street, NW

Washington, DC 20037

Tel: 202-785-1614

Email: fba@fedbar.org

http://fedbar.org

For information on choosing a law school, law careers, salaries, and alternative law careers, contact

National Association for Law Placement

1025 Connecticut Avenue, NW, Suite 1110

Washington, DC 20036-5413

Tel: 202-835-1001

Email: info@nalp.org

http://www.nalp.org

HOW TO BECOME A FEDERAL OR STATE OFFICIAL

THE JOB

The decisions of state and federal lawmakers affect your daily life and your future. State and federal officials pass laws concerning the arts, education, taxes, employment, health care, and other areas in efforts to change and improve communities and standards of living.

Besides the *president* and *vice president* of the United States, the executive branch of the national government consists of the president's cabinet, including, among others, the secretaries of state, treasury, defense, interior, agriculture, homeland security, and health and human services. These officials are appointed by the president and approved by the Senate. The members of the Office of Management and Budget, the Council of Economic Advisors, and the National Security Council are also executive officers of the national government.

Nearly every state's governing body resembles that of the federal government. Just as the U.S. Congress is composed of the Senate and the House of Representatives, each state (with one exception, Nebraska) has a senate and a house. The executive branch of the U.S. government is headed by the president and vice president, while the states elect governors and lieutenant governors. The *governor* is the chief executive officer of a state. In all states, a large government administration handles a variety of functions related to agriculture, highway and motor vehicle supervision, public safety and corrections, regulation of intrastate business and industry, and some aspects of education, public health, and welfare. The governor's job is to manage this administration. Some states also have a *lieutenant governor,* who serves as the presiding officer of the state's senate. Other elected officials commonly include a secretary of state, state treasurer, state auditor, attorney general, and superintendent of public instruction.

State senators and *state representatives* are the legislators elected to represent the districts and regions of cities and counties within the state. The number of members of a state's legislature varies from state to state. In the U.S. Congress, there are 100 senators (as established by the Constitution—two senators from each state) and 435 representatives. The number of representatives each state is allowed to send to the U.S. Congress varies based on the state's population as determined by the national census. Based on results from Census 2000, California is the most populous state and sends the most representatives (53). The primary function of all legislators, at both the state and national levels, is to make laws. With a staff of aides, senators and representatives attempt to learn as much as they can about the bills being considered. They research legislation, prepare reports, meet constituents and interest groups, speak to the press, and discuss and debate legislation on the floor of the House or Senate. Legislators also may be involved in selecting other members of the government, supervising the government administration, appropriating funds, impeaching executive and judicial officials, and determining election procedures, among other activities. A state legislator may be involved in examining such situations as the state's relationship to Native American tribes, the level of school violence, and welfare reform.

"Time in each day goes by so quickly," says Don Preister, who serves on the state legislature in Nebraska, "there's no time to read up on all legislation and all the information the constituents send in." Nebraska is the only state with a single-house system. When the state Senate is in session, Preister commits many hours to discussing and debating issues with other state senators and gathering information on proposed legislation. In addition to attending Senate sessions, Preister attends committee hearings. His committees include Natural Resources and Urban Affairs. "A hearing lasts from 20 minutes to three or four hours," he says, "depending on the intensity of the issues." Despite having to devote about 60 hours a week to the job when the Senate is in session, Preister finds his work a wonderful opportunity to be of service to the community and to improve lives. "I take a lot of personal satisfaction from being a voice for people whose voices aren't often heard in government."

REQUIREMENTS
High School
Courses in government, civics, and history will give you an understanding of the structure of state and federal governments. English courses are important because you need good writing skills for communicating with constituents and other government officials. Math and accounting help you to develop the analytical skills needed for examining statistics and demographics. You should take science courses because you will be making decisions concerning health, medicine, and technological advances. Journalism

classes will help you learn about the print and broadcast media and the role they play in politics.

Postsecondary Training

State and federal legislators come from all walks of life. Some hold master's degrees and doctorates, while others have only high school educations. Although a majority of government officials hold law degrees, others have undergraduate or graduate degrees in such areas as journalism, economics, political science, history, and English. Regardless of your major as an undergraduate, it is important to take classes in English literature, statistics, foreign language, Western civilization, and economics. Graduate studies can focus more on one area of study; some prospective government officials pursue master's degrees in public administration or international affairs. Consider participating in an internship program that will involve you with local and state officials. Contact the offices of your state legislators and of your state's members of Congress to apply for internships directly.

Other Requirements

"You should have concern for people," Don Preister says. "You should have an ability to listen and understand people and their concerns." Paying attention to the needs of communities should be of foremost importance to anyone pursuing a government office. Although historically some politicians have had questionable purposes in their campaigns for office, most successful politicians are devoted to making positive changes and improvements. Good social skills will help you make connections, get elected, and make things happen once in office. You should also enjoy argument, debate, and opposition—you will get a lot of it as you attempt to get laws passed. A good temperament in such situations will earn you the respect of your colleagues. Strong character and a good background will help you avoid the personal attacks that occasionally accompany government office.

EXPLORING

If you are 16 or older, you can gain experience in a legislature. The U.S. Congress and possibly your state legislature offer opportunities for young adults who have demonstrated a commitment to government study to work as *pages*. For Congress, pages run messages across Capitol Hill and have the opportunity to see senators and representatives debating and discussing bills. The length of a page's service can be for one summer or up to one year. Contact your state's senator or representative for an application.

You can also explore government careers by becoming involved with local elections. Many candidates for local and state offices welcome young people to assist with campaigns. You might be asked to make calls, post signs, or hand out information about the candidate. Not only will you get to see the politician at work, but you will meet others with an interest in government.

Another great way to learn about government is to become involved in an issue of interest to you. Participate with a grassroots advocacy group or read about the bills up for vote in the state legislature and U.S. Congress. When you feel strongly about an issue and are well educated on the subject, contact the offices of state legislators and members of Congress to express your views. Visit the websites of the House and Senate and of your state legislature to read about bills, schedules, and the legislators. The National Conference of State Legislators (NCSL) also hosts a website (www.ncsl.org) featuring legislative news and links to state legislatures.

EMPLOYERS

State legislators work for the state government, and many hold other jobs as well. Because of the part-time nature of some legislative offices, state legislators may hold part-time jobs or own their own businesses. Federal officials work full-time for the Senate, the House, or the executive branch.

STARTING OUT

There is no direct career path for state and federal officials. Some enter their positions after some success with political activism on the grassroots level. Others work their way up from local government positions to state legislature and into federal office. Those who serve as U.S. Congress members have worked in the military, journalism, academia, business, and many other fields.

Many politicians get their start by assisting someone else's campaign or by advocating an issue. Don Preister's beginnings with the Nebraska state legislature are particularly inspiring. Because of his involvement in grassroots organizing to improve his neighborhood, he was encouraged by friends and neighbors to run for senator of the district. Others, however, believed he would never get elected running against a man who had had a lot of political success, as well as great finances to back his campaign. "I didn't have any money," Preister says, "or any experience in campaigning. So I went door-to-door to meet the people of the district. I went to every house and apartment in the district." He won that election in 1992 and won again in 1996 and 2000.

ADVANCEMENT

Initiative is one key to success in politics. Advancement can be rapid for a fast learner who is independently motivated, but a career in politics most often takes a long time to establish. Most state and federal officials start by pursuing training and work experience in their particular field, while getting involved in politics at the local level. Many people progress from local politics to state politics. It is not uncommon for a state legislator to eventually run for a seat in Congress. Appointees to the president's cabinet and presidential and vice presidential candidates frequently have held positions in Congress.

EARNINGS

In general, salaries for government officials tend to be lower than what the official could make working in the private sector. In the case of state legislators, the pay can be significantly lower.

The Bureau of Labor Statistics reports that the median annual earning of government legislators was $14,650 in 2001. Salaries generally ranged from less than $11,830 to more than $64,890, although some officials earn nothing at all.

According to the NCSL, state legislators make from $10,000 to $47,000 a year. A few states, however, do not pay state legislators anything other than an expense allowance. But a state's executive officials get paid better: *The Book of the States* lists salaries of state governors as ranging from $60,000 in Arkansas to a high of $130,000 in New York.

In 2001 U.S. senators and representatives earned $145,100; the Senate and House majority and minority leaders earned $161,200; the vice president was paid $186,300; and the president earned $400,000.

Congressional leaders such as the Speaker of the House and the Senate majority leader receive higher salaries than the other Congress members. The Speaker of the House makes $186,300 a year. United States Congress members receive excellent insurance, vacation, and other benefits.

WORK ENVIRONMENT

Most government officials work in a typical office setting. Some may work a regular 40-hour week, while others will typically work long hours and weekends. One potential drawback to political life, particularly for the candidate running for office, is that there is no real off-duty time. One is continually under observation by the press and public, and the personal lives of candidates and office-holders are discussed frequently in the media.

Because these officials must be appointed or elected in order to keep their jobs, the ability to determine long-range job objectives is slim. There may be extended periods of unemployment, when living off of savings or working at other jobs may be necessary.

Frequent travel is involved in campaigning and in holding office, so some people with children may find the lifestyle demanding on their families.

OUTLOOK

The U.S. Department of Labor predicts that employment of federal and state officials will grow about as fast as the average through 2010. To attract more candidates to run for legislative offices, states may consider salary increases and better benefits for state senators and representatives.

But changes in pay and benefits for federal officials are unlikely. An increase in the number of representatives is possible as the U.S. population grows, but would require additional office space and other costly expansions. For the most part, the structures of state and federal legislatures will remain unchanged, although the topic of limiting the number of terms that a representative is allowed to serve does often arise in election years.

The federal government has made efforts to shift costs to the states; if this continues, it could change the way state legislatures and executive officers operate with regard to public funding. Already, welfare reform has resulted in state governments looking for financial aid in handling welfare cases and job programs. Arts funding may also become the sole responsibility of the states as the National Endowment for the Arts loses support from Congress.

With the government's commitment to developing a place on the Internet, contacting your state and federal representatives, learning about legislation, and organizing grassroots advocacy have become much easier. Voter awareness of candidates, public policy issues, and legislation will increase and may affect how future representatives make decisions. Also look for government programming to be part of cable television's expansion into digital broadcasting. New modes of communication will allow constituents to become even more involved in the actions of their representatives.

TO LEARN MORE ABOUT FEDERAL AND STATE OFFICIALS

BOOKS

Axelrod-Contrada, Joan, and John Kerry. *Career Opportunities in Politics, Government, and Activism.* New York: Facts On File, 2003.

Camenson, Blythe. *Real People Working in Government. (On the Job Series.)* New York: McGraw-Hill, 1998.

Georgetown University School of Foreign Service. *Careers in International Affairs.* 7th ed. Washington, D.C.: Georgetown University Press, 2003.

Ginsberg, Benjamin, et al. *We the People: An Introduction to American Politics*. New York: Norton, 2003.

Woll, Peter, ed. *American Government: Readings and Cases.* 13th ed. Boston: Addison-Wesley, 1998.

ORGANIZATIONS

Visit the Senate and House websites for extensive information about Congress, government history, current legislation, and links to state legislature sites.

U.S. Senate

Office of Senator (Name)

United States Senate

Washington, DC 20510

202-224-3121

www.senate.gov

U.S. House of Representatives

Office of the Honorable (Name)

Washington, DC 20515

202-224-3121

www.house.gov

To read about state legislatures, policy issues, legislative news, and other related information, visit the NCSL's website.

National Conference of State Legislatures (NCSL)

444 North Capitol Street, NW, Suite 515

Washington, DC 20001

202-624-5400

www.ncsl.org

TO LEARN MORE ABOUT HILLARY RODHAM CLINTON

BOOKS

Brock, David. *The Seduction of Hillary Rodham.* New York: The Free Press, 1996.

Clinton, Hillary Rodham. *An Invitation to the White House: At Home with History.* New York: Simon & Schuster, 2000.

———. *Dear Socks, Dear Buddy: Kids' Letters to the First Pets.* New York: Simon & Schuster, 1998.

———. *It Takes A Village and Other Lessons Children Teach Us.* New York: Simon & Schuster, 1996.

———. *Living History*. New York: Simon & Schuster, 2003.

Conason, Joe and Gene Lyons. *The Hunting of the President: The Ten-Year Campaign to Destroy Bill and Hillary Clinton*. New York: St. Martin's, 2000.

Gross, Martin Louis. *The Great Whitewater Fiasco: An American Tale of Money, Power, and Politics*. New York: Ballantine, 1994.

Keniston, Kenneth. *Carnegie Council on Children: All Our Children*. New York: Harcourt, 1978.

Lyons, Gene. *Fools for Scandal: How the Media Invented Whitewater*. New York: Harper's Magazine Foundation, 1996.

Milton, Joyce. *The First Partner: Hillary Rodham Clinton*. New York: William Morrow and Company, Inc., 1999.

Morris, Roger. *Partners in Power: The Clintons and Their America*. New York: Henry Holt, 1996.

Olson, Barbara. *Hell to Pay: The Unfolding Story of Hillary Rodham Clinton*. Washington: Regnery Publishing, Inc., 1999.

Radcliffe, Donnie. *Hillary Rodham Clinton: A First Lady for Our Time*. New York: Warner Books, Inc., 1993.

Sheehy, Gail. *Hillary's Choice*. New York: Ballantine Books, 1999, 2000.

Stewart, James B. *Blood Sport: The President and His Adversaries*. New York: Simon & Schuster, 1996.

Tomasky, Michael. *Hillary's Turn: Inside Her Improbable, Victorious Senate Campaign.* New York: The Free Press (Simon & Schuster), 2001.

Toobin, Jeffrey. *A Vast Conspiracy: The Real Story of the Sex Scandal That Nearly Brought Down a President.* New York: Random House, 2000.

INTERNET SOURCES

"About Senator Hillary Rodham Clinton," Senator Clinton website. Available online. URL:http://clinton.senate.gov/about_hrc.html. Downloaded May 29, 2003.

"Clintons urge caution on action against Iraq," CNN website. Available online. URL:http://www.cnn.com/2002/ALLPOLITICS/08/31/clinton.iraq/index.html. Posted on August 31, 2002.

"Hillary Rodham Clinton: First Lady of the United States. . .and a woman who loves to help children," Women's International Center website. Available online. URL: http://www.wic.org/bio/hclinton.htm. Downloaded May 29, 2003.

"Hillary Rodham Clinton," First Lady Biographies, White House website. Available online. URL: http://www.whitehouse.gov/history/firstladies/text/hc42.html. Downloaded May 29, 2003.

"Independent Counsel Robert Ray's statement on Whitewater," CNN website. Available online. URL:

http://www.cnn.com/2000/ALLPOLITICS/stories/ 09/20/whitewater/ray.html. Posted on September 20, 2000.

"Poll: Hillary Clinton top Democratic 2004 choice," CNN website. Available online. URL: http://www.cnn.com/ ALLPOLITICS/12/21/hillary.poll. Posted on December 21, 2002.

CNN *Crossfire:* Interview with Senator Hillary Rodham Clinton (transcript of program aired July 9, 2003). Available online. URL: http://www.cnn.com/TRAN-SCRIPTS/0307/09/cf.00.html. Downloaded on August 18, 2003.

Ferguson, Sarah. "Students Protest Senator Clinton's Decision to Back Bush's War Plans." *The Village Voice* website. Available online. URL: http://www.villagevoice. com/print/issues/0242/ferguson.php. Posted on October 15, 2002.

Goldstein, David. "House panel reviewing Clintons' gifts sees system to fix," *The Philadelphia Inquirer* website. Available online. URL: http://www.philly.com/mld/ inquirer/news/nation/2661213.html. Posted on February 13, 2002.

Hernandez, Raymond. "Book Gives Mrs. Clinton A New Turn in Spotlight," *The New York Times*. June 9, 2003.

Hirschkorn, Phil (producer). "Senator Clinton offers preview of first bill," CNN website. Available online. URL:

http://www.cnn.com/2001/ALLPOLITICS/02/19/
hillary.economic.pla/index.html. Posted on February
20, 2001.

Hirschkorn, Phil. "Sen. Clinton asks shoulder-fired missile
defense," CNN website. Available online. URL:
http://www.cnn.com/2002/ALLPOLITICS/12/02/
clinton.missiles/index.html. Posted on December 3, 2002.

Kirkpatrick, David D. "For Mrs. Clinton, One Day, 200,000
Copies," *The New York Times*. June 11, 2003.

Lancaster, John. "Clinton: Damage 'Incalculable'," *The
Washington Post*. Available online. URL:http://www.wash-
ingtonpost.com/ac2/wp-dyn/A40105-2001Oct10.html.
October 11, 2001.

Marks, Alexandra. "Clinton's switch from state dinners to
sewers," *The Christian Science Monitor* website. Available
online. URL: http://www.csmonitor.com/2001/0822/
p2s1-uspo.html. Posted on August 22, 2001.

VandeHei, Jim. "Clinton Develops Into a Force in the
Senate," *The Washington Post* website. Available online.
URL:http://www.washingtonpost.com/ac2/wp-wyn/
A42590-2003Mar4.html. Posted on March 5, 2003.

Weeks, Linton. "Sen. Clinton's White House Memoir to Hit
Stores In June," *The Washington Post* website. Available
online. URL:http://www.washingtonpost.com/ac2/
wp-dyn/A51539-2003Apr29.html. Posted on April 29,
2003.

INDEX

149

ABOUT THE AUTHOR

Bernard Ryan Jr., has authored, coauthored, or ghost-written 30 books in such topics as biography, early childhood education, community service for teens, career guides in the fields of advertising and journalism, courtroom trials, personal financial planning and the Ferguson Career Biography *Condoleezza Rice: National Security Advisor and Musician*. His *Tyler's Titanic* is an early chapter book about what happens when a boy finds a way to visit the wreckage of the great ship on the ocean floor. In *The Wright Brothers: Inventors of the Airplane*, he tells the sixth- to ninth-grade reader the Wrights' life stories and explains how they brought the world the miracle of flight. His *Helping Your Child Start School* is an introduction to kindergarten for parents. *Simple Ways to Help Your Kids Become Dollar-Smart*, coauthored with financial planner Elizabeth Lewin, helps parents teach children, ages seven to 18, how to handle money. His *The Poisoned Life of Mrs. Maybrick* is the biography of an American woman in Liverpool, England, in 1889, who was the defendant in one of history's great murder trials. Mr. Ryan has written many shorter pieces for magazine and newspaper publication and is a graduate of The Rectory School, Kent School, and Princeton University. A native of Albion, New York, he lives with his wife, Jean Bramwell Ryan, in Southbury, Connecticut. They have two daughters and two grandchildren.